ARTEMUS WARD,

HIS BOOK,

MR. WARD DELIVERING HIS GREAT UNION SPEECH. [*See Page* 209.]

HIS BOOK

WITH MANY COMIC ILLUSTRATIONS.

NEW-YORK:

CARLETON, PUBLISHER,

[LATE RUDD & CARLETON]

MDCCCLXII.

To

CHARLES W. COE, Esq.,

OF CLEVELAND, OHIO,

(A Friend all the Year Round,

This Book is Dedicated

CONTENTS.

MISCELLANEOUS.

NEW ENGLAND RUM, AND ITS EFFECTS. [*See Page* 214.]

LIST OF ILLUSTRATIONS.

At the Door of the Tent.

Ladies and Gentlemen, the Show is about to commence. You could not well expect to go in without paying, but you may pay without going in. I can say no fairer than that.

ARTEMUS WARD

ONE OF MR. WARD'S BUSINESS LETTERS.

To the Editor of the ———

SIR — I'm movin along — slowly along — down tords your place. I want you should rite me a letter, sayin how is the show bizniss in your place. My show at present consists of three moral Bares, a Kangaroo (a amoozin little Raskal — t'would make you larf yerself to deth to see the little cuss jump up and squeal) wax figgers of G. Washington Gen. Tayler John Bunyan Capt. Kidd and Dr. Webster in the act of killin Dr. Parkman, besides several miscellanyus moral wax statoots of celebrated piruts & murderers, &c., ekalled by few & exceld by none. Now Mr. Editor, scratch orf a few lines sayin how is the show bizniss down to your place. I shall hav my hanbills dun at your offiss. Depend upon it. I want you should git my hanbills up in flamin stile. Also git up a tremenjus excitemunt in yr. paper 'bowt my onparaleld Show. We must fetch the public sumhow. We must wurk on their feelins. Cum the moral on 'em strong. If it's a temprance community tell 'em I sined the pledge fifteen minits arter Ise born, but on the contery ef your peple take their tods, say Mister Ward is as Jenial a feller as we ever met, full of conwiviality, & the life an sole of the Soshul Bored. Take, don't you? If you say anythin abowt my show say my snaiks is as harmliss as the new born Babe. What a interestin study it is to see a zewological animil like a snaik under perfeck subjecshun! My kangaroo is the most larfable little cuss I ever saw. All for 15 cents. I am anxyus to skewer your infloounce. I repeet in regard to them hanbills that I shall git 'em struck orf up to your printin office. My perlitercal sentiments agree with yourn exackly. I know thay do, becawz I never saw a man whoos didn't.

Respectively yures,

A. Ward.

P. S. — You scratch my back & Ile scratch your back.

THE SHAKERS.

The Shakers is the strangest religious sex I ever met. I'd hearn tell of 'em and I'd seen 'em, with their broad brim'd hats and long wastid coats; but I'd never cum into immejit contack with 'em, and I'd sot 'em down as lackin intelleck, as I'd never seen 'em to my Show — leastways, if they cum they was disgised in white peple's close, so I didn't know 'em.

But in the Spring of 18 —, I got swampt in the exterior of New York State, one dark and stormy night, when the winds Blue pityusly, and I was forced to tie up with the Shakers.

I was toilin threw the mud, when in the dim vister of the futer I obsarved the gleams of a taller candle. Tiein a hornet's nest to my off hoss's tail to kinder encourage him, I soon reached the place.

ARTEMUS AMONG THE SHAKERS. "YAY," THEY SED, AND I YAY'D. [*See Page* 28.]

I knockt at the door, which it was opened unto me by a tall, slick-faced, solum lookin individooal, who turn'd out to be a Elder.

"Mr. Shaker," sed I, "you see before you a Babe in the Woods, so to speak, and he axes shelter of you."

"Yay," sed the Shaker, and he led the way into the house, another Shaker bein sent to put my hosses and waggin under kiver.

A solum female, lookin sumwhat like a last year's bean-pole stuck into a long meal bag, cum in and axed me was I athurst and did I hunger? to which I urbanely anserd "a few." She went orf and I endeverd to open a conversashun with the old man.

"Elder, I spect?" sed I.

"Yay," he sed.

"Helth's good, I reckon?"

"Yay."

"What's the wages of a Elder, when he understans his bizness — or do you devote your sarvices gratooitus?"

"Yay."

"Stormy night, sir."

"Yay."

"If the storm continners there'll be a mess underfoot, hay?"

"Yay."

"It's onpleasant when there's a mess underfoot?"

"Yay."

"If I may be so bold, kind sir, what's the price of that pecooler kind of weskit you wear, incloodin trimmins?"

"Yay!"

I pawsd a minit, and then, thinkin I'd be faseshus with him and see how that would go, I slapt him on the shoulder, bust into a harty larf, and told him that as a *yayer* he had no livin ekal.

He jumpt up as if Bilin water had bin squirted into his ears, groaned, rolled his eyes up tords the sealin and sed: "You're a man of sin!" He then walkt out of the room.

Jest then the female in the meal bag stuck her hed into the room and statid that refreshments awaited the weary travler, and I sed if it was vittles she ment, the weary travler was agreeable, and I follered her into the next room.

I sot down to the table and the female in the meal bag pored out sum tea. She sed nothin, and for five minutes the only live thing in that room was a old wooden clock, which tickt in a subdood and bashful manner in the corner. This dethly stillness made me oneasy, and I determined to talk to the female or bust. So sez I, "marrige is agin your rules, I bleeve, marm?"

"Yay."

"The sexes liv strickly apart, I spect?"

"Yay."

"It's kinder singler," sez I, puttin on my most sweetest look and speakin in a winnin voice, "that so fair a made as thou never got hitched to some likely feller." [N. B. — She was upards of 40 and homely as a stump fence, but I thawt I'd tickil her.]

"I don't like men!" she sed, very short.

"Wall, I dunno," sez I, "they're a rayther

important part of the populashun. I don't scacely see how we could git along without 'em."

"Us poor wimin folks would git along a grate deal better if there was no men!"

"You'll excoos me, marm, but I dont think that air would work. It wouldn't be regler."

"I'm fraid of men!" she sed.

"That's onnecessary, marm. *You* ain't in no danger. Don't fret yourself on that pint."

"Here we're shot out from the sinful world. Here all is peas. Here we air brothers and sisters. We don't marry and consekently we hav no domestic difficulties. Husbans don't abooze their wives — wives don't worrit their husbans. There's no children here to worrit us. Nothin to worrit us here. No wicked matrimony here. Would thow like to be a Shaker?"

"No," sez I, "it ain't my stile."

I had now histed in as big a load of pervishuns as I could carry comfortable, and, leanin back in my cheer, commenst pickin my teeth with a fork. The female went out, leavin me all alone with the clock.

I hadn't sot thar long before the Elder poked his hed in at the door. "You're a man of sin!" he sed, and groaned and went away.

Direckly thar cum in two young Shakeresses, as putty and slick lookin gals as I ever met. It is troo they was drest in meal bags like the old one I'd met previsly, and their shiny, silky har was hid from sight by long white caps, sich as I spose female Josts wear; but their eyes sparkled like diminds, their cheeks was like roses, and they was charmin enuff to make a man throw stuns at his granmother, if they axed him to. They commenst clearin away the dishes, castin shy glances at me all the time. I got excited. I forgot Betsy Jane in my rapter, and sez I, "my pretty dears, how air you?"

"We air well," they solumly sed.

"Whar's the old man?" sed I, in a soft voice.

"Of whom dost thow speak — Brother Uriah?"

"I mean the gay and festiv cuss who calls me a man of sin. Shouldn't wonder if his name was Uriah."

"He has retired."

"Wall, my pretty dears," sez I, "let's hav sum fun. Let's play puss in the corner. What say?"

"Air you a Shaker, sir?" they axed.

"Wall, my pretty dears, I haven't arrayed my proud form in a long weskit yit, but if they was all like you perhaps I'd jine 'em As it is, I'm a Shaker pro-temporary."

They was full of fun. I seed that at fust, only they was a leetle skeery. I tawt 'em Puss in the corner and sich like plase, and we had a nice time, keepin quiet of course so the old man shouldn't hear. When we broke up, sez I, "my pretty dears, ear I go you hav no objections, hav you, to a innersent kiss at partin?"

"Yay," thay sed, and I *yay'd.*

I went up stairs to bed. I spose I'd bin snoozin half a hour when I was woke up by a noise at the door. I sot up in bed, leanin on my elbers and rubbin my eyes, and I saw the follerin picter: The Elder stood in the doorway, with a taller candle in his hand. He hadn't no wearin appeerel on except his night close, which flutterd in the breeze like a

Seseshun flag. He sed, "You're a man of sin!" then groaned and went away.

I went to sleep agin, and drempt of runnin orf with the pretty little Shakeresses, mounted on my Californy Bar. I thawt the Bar insisted on steerin strate for my dooryard in Baldinsville and that Betsy Jane cum out and giv us a warm recepshun with a panfull of Bilin water. I was woke up arly by the Elder. He sed refreshments was reddy for me down stairs. Then sayin I was a man of sin, he went groanin away.

As I was goin threw the entry to the room where the vittles was, I cum across the Elder and the old female I'd met the night before, and what d'ye spose they was up to? Huggin and kissin like young lovers in their gushingist state. Sez I, "my Shaker frends, I reckon you'd better suspend the rules, and git marrid!"

"You must excoos Brother Uriah," sed the female; "he's subjeck to fits and hain't got no command over hisself when he's into 'em."

"Sartinly," sez I, "I've bin took that way myself frequent."

"You're a man of sin!" sed the Elder.

Arter breakfust my little Shaker frends cum in agin to clear away the dishes.

"My pretty dears," sez I, "shall we *yay* agin?"

"Nay," they sed, and I *nay'd*.

The Shakers axed me to go to their meetin, as they was to hav sarvices that mornin, so I put on a clean biled rag and went. The meetin house was as neat as a pin. The floor was white as chalk and smooth as glass. The Shakers was all on hand, in clean weskits and meal bags, ranged on the floor like milingtery companies, the mails on one side of the room and the females on tother. They commenst clappin their hands and singin and dancin. They danced kinder slow at fust, but as they got warmed up they shaved it down very brisk, I tell you. Elder Uriah, in particler, exhiberted a right smart chance of spryness in his legs, considerin his time of life, and as he cum a dubble shuffle near where I sot, I rewarded him with a approvin smile and sed: "Hunky boy! Go it, my gay and festiv cuss!"

"You're a man of sin!" he sed, continnerin his shuffle.

The Sperret, as they called it, then moved a short fat Shaker to say a few remarks. He sed they was Shakers and all was ekal. They was the purest and seleckest peple on the yearth. Other peple was sinful as they could be, but Shakers was all right. Shakers was all goin kerslap to the Promist Land, and nobody want goin to stand at the gate to bar 'em out, if they did they'd git run over.

The Shakers then danced and sung agin, and arter they was threw, one of 'em axed me what I thawt of it.

Sez I, "What duz it siggerfy?"

"What?" sez he.

"Why this jumpin up and singin? This long weskit bizniss, and this anty-matrimony idee? My frends, you air neat and tidy. Your lands is flowin with milk and honey. Your brooms is fine, and your apple sass is honest. When a man buys a kag of apple sass of you he don't find a grate many shavins under a few layers of sass — a little Game I'm sorry to say sum of my New Englan ancesters used to practiss. Your garding seeds is fine, and if I should sow 'em on the rock of Gibralter probly I should raise a good mess of garding sass. You air honest in your dealins. You air quiet and don't distarb nobody. For all this I givs you credit. But your religion is small pertaters, I must say. You mope away your lives here in single retchidness, and as you air all by yourselves nothing ever conflicks with your pecooler idees, except when Human Nater busts out among you, as I understan she sumtimes do. [I giv Uriah a sly wink here, which made the old feller squirm like a speared Eel.] You wear long weskits and long faces, and lead a gloomy life indeed. No children's prattle is ever hearn around your harthstuns — you air in a dreary fog all the time, and you treat the jolly sunshine of life as tho' it was a thief, drivin it from your doors by them weskits, and meal bags, and pecooler noshuns of yourn. The gals among you, sum of which air as slick pieces of caliker as

I ever sot eyes on, air syin to place their heds agin weskits which kiver honest, manly harts, while you old heds fool yerselves with the idee that they air fulfillin their mishun here, and air contented. Here you air, all pend up by yerselves, talkin about the sins of a world you don't know nothin of. Meanwhile said world continners to resolve round on her own axeltree onct in every 24 hours, subjeck to the Constitution of the United States, and is a very plesant place of residence. It's a unnatral, onreasonable and dismal life you're leadin here. So it strikes me. My Shaker frends, I now bid you a welcome adoo. You hav treated me exceedin well. Thank you kindly, one and all.

"A base exhibiter of depraved monkeys and onprincipled wax works!" sed Uriah.

"Hello, Uriah," sez I, "I'd most forgot you. Wall, look out for them fits of yourn, and don't catch cold and die in the flour of your youth and beauty."

And I resoomed my jerney.

HIGH-HANDED OUTRAGE AT UTICA.

In the Faul of 1856, I showed my show in Utiky, a trooly grate sitty in the State of New York.

The people gave me a cordyal recepshun. The press was loud in her prases.

1 day as I was givin a descripshun of my Beests and Snaiks in my usual flowry stile what was my skorn & disgust to see a big burly feller walk up to the cage containin my wax figgers of the Lord's Last Supper, and cease Judas Iscarrot by the feet and drag him out on the ground. He then commenced fur to pound him as hard as he cood.

"What under the son are you abowt?" cried I.

Sez he, "What did you bring this pussylanermus cuss here fur?" & he hit the wax figger another tremenjis blow on the hed.

Sez I, "You egrejus ass, that air's a wax figger — a representashun of the false 'Postle."

Sez he, "That's all very well fur you to say but I tell you, old man, that Judas Iscarrot can't show hisself in Utiky with impunerty by a darn site!" with which observashun he kaved in Judassis hed. The young man belonged to 1 of the first famerlies in Utiky. I sood him, and the Joory brawt in a verdick of Arson in the 3d degree.

CELEBRATION AT BALDINSVILLE IN HONOR OF THE ATLANTIC CABLE.

Baldinsville, Injianny, Sep the onct, 18&58.— I was summund home from Cinsinnaty quite suddin by a lettur from the Supervizers of Baldinsville, sayin as how grate things was on the Tappis in that air town in refferunse to sellebratin the compleshun of the Sub-Mershine Tellergraph & axkin me to be Pressunt. Lockin up my Kangeroo and wax wurks in a sekure stile I took my departer for Baldinsville — "my own, my nativ lan," which I gut intwo at early kandle litin on the follerin night & just as the sellerbrashun and illumernashun ware commensin.

Baldinsville was trooly in a blaze of glory. Near can I forgit the surblime speckticul which met my gase as I alited from the Staige with my umbreller and verlise. The Tarvern was lit up with taller kandles all over & a grate bon fire was burnin in frunt thareof. A Transpirancy was tied onto the sine post with the follerin wurds — " Giv us Liberty or Deth." Old Tompkinsis grosery was illumernated with 5 tin lantuns and the follerin Transpirancy was in the winder — " The Sub-Mershine Tellergraph & the Baldinsville and Stonefield Plank Road — the 2 grate eventz of the 19th centerry — may intestines strife never mar their grandjure." Simpkinsis shoe shop was all ablase with kandles and lantuns. A American Eagle was painted onto a flag in a winder — also these wurds, viz — " The Constitooshun must be Presarved." The Skool house was lited up in grate stile and the winders was filld with mottoes amung which I notised the follerin — " Trooth smashed to erth shall rize agin — YOU CAN'T STOP HER." " The Boy stood on the Burnin Deck whense awl but him had Fled." " Prokrastinashun is the theaf of Time." " Be virtoous & you will be Happy." " Intemperunse has cawsed a heap of trubble — shun the Bo'e," an the follerin sentimunt written by the skool master, who graduated at Hudson Kollige. "Baldinsville sends greetin to Her Magisty the Queen, & hopes all hard feelins which has heretofore previs bin felt between the Supervizers of Baldinsville and the British Parlimunt, if such there has been, may now be forever wiped frum our Escutchuns. Baldinsville this night rejoises over the gerlorious event which sementz 2 grate nashuns onto one anuther by means of a elecktric wire under the roarin billers of the Nasty Deep. QUOSQUE TANTRUM, A BUTTER, CATERLINY, PATENT NOSTRUM!" Squire Smith's house was lited up regardlis of expense. His little sun William Henry stood upon the roof firin orf crackers. The old 'Squire hisself was dressed up in soljer clothes and stood on his door-step, pintin his sword sollumly to a American flag which was suspendid on top of a pole in frunt of his house. Frequiently he wood take orf his cocked hat & wave it round in a impressive stile. His oldest darter Mis Isabeller Smith, who has just cum home from the Perkinsville Female Intertoot, appeared at the frunt winder in the West room as the goddis of liberty, & sung "I see them on their windin way." Booteus 1, sed I to myself, you air a angil & nothin shorter. N. Boneparte Smith, the 'Squire's oldest sun, drest hisself up as Venus the God of Wars and red the Decleration of Inderpendunse from the left chambir winder. The 'Squire's wife didn't jine in the festiverties. She sed it was the tarnulest nonsense she ever seed. Sez she to the 'Squire, "Cum into the house and go to bed you old fool, you. Tomorrer you'll be goin round half-ded with the rumertism & won't gin us a minit's peace till you get well." Sez the 'Squire "Betsy, you little appresiate the importance of the event which I this night commemerate." Sez she, "Commemerate a cat's tail—cum into the house this instant, you pesky old critter." "Betsy," sez the 'Squire, wavin his sword, "retire." This made her just as mad as she could stick. She retired, but cum out agin putty quick with a panfull of Bilin hot water which she throwed all over the 'Squire, & Surs, you wood have split your sides larfin to see the old man jump up and holler & run into the house. Except this unpropishus circumstance all went as merry as a carriage bell, as Lord Byrun sez. Doctor Hutchinsis offiss was likewise lited up and a Transpirancy on which was painted the Queen in the act of drinkin sum of "Hutchinsis invigorater," was stuck into one of the winders. The Baldinsville Bugle of Liberty noospaper offiss was also illumernated, & the follerin mottoes stuck out — "The Press is the Arkermejian leaver which moves the world." "Vote Early." "Buckle on your Armer." "Now is the time to Subscribe." "Franklin, Morse & Field." "Terms $1,50 a year — liberal reducshuns to clubs." In short the villige of Baldinsville was in a perfect fewroar. I never seed so many peple thar befour in my born days. Ile not attemp to describe the seens of that grate night. Wurds wood fale me ef I shood try to do it. I shall stop here a few periods and enjoy my "Oatem cum dig the tates," as our skool master obsarves, in the buzzum of my famerly, & shall then resume the show bisnis, which Ive bin into twenty two (22) yeres and six (6) months.

AMONG THE SPIRITS.

My naburs is mourn harf crazy on the new fangled idear about Sperrets. Sperretooul Sircles is held nitely & 4 or 5 long hared fellers has settled here and gone into the sperret biznis excloosively. A atemt was made to git Mrs. A. Ward to embark into the Sperret biznis but the atemt faled. 1 of the long hared fellers told her she was a ethereal creeter & wood make a sweet mejium, whareupon she attact him with a mop handle & drove him out of the house. I will hear obsarve that Mrs. Ward is a invalerble womun — the partner of my goys & the shairer of my sorrers. In my absunse she watchis my interests & things with a Eagle Eye & when I return she welcums me in afectionate stile. Trooly it is with us as it was with Mr. & Mrs. INGOMER in the Play, to whit —

2 soles with but a single thawt
2 harts which beet as 1.

My naburs injooced me to attend a Sperretooul Sircle at Squire Smith's. When I arrove I found the east room chock full includin all the old maids in the villige & the long hared fellers a4sed. When I went in I was salootid with "hear cums the benited man" — "hear cums the hory-heded unbeleever" — "hear cums the skoffer at trooth," etsettery, etsettery.

Sez I, "my frens, it's troo I'm hear, & now bring on your Sperrets."

1 of the long hared fellers riz up and sed he would state a few remarks. He sed man was a critter of intelleck & was movin on to a Gole. Sum men had bigger intellecks than other men had and thay wood git to the Gole the soonerest. Sum men was beests & wood never git into the Gole at all. He sed the Erth was materiel but man was immaterial, and hens man was different from the Erth. The Erth, continnered the speaker, resolves round on its own axeltree onct in 24 hours, but as man haint gut no axeltree he cant resolve. He sed the ethereal essunce of the koordinate branchis

of superhuman natur becum mettymorfussed as man progrest in harmonial coexistunce & eventooally anty humanized theirselves & turned into reglar sperretuellers. [This was versifferusly applauded by the cumpany, and as I make it a pint to get along as pleasant as possible, I sung out "bully for you, old boy."]

The cumpany then drew round the table and the Sircle kommenst to go it. Thay axed me if thare was anbody in the Sperret land which I wood like to convarse with. I sed if Bill Tompkins, who was onct my partner in the show biznis, was sober, I should like to convarse with him a few periods.

"Is the Sperret of William Tompkins present?" sed 1 of the long hared chaps, and there was three knox on the table.

Sez I, "William, how goze it, Old Sweetness?"

"Pretty ruff, old hoss," he replide.

That was a pleasant way we had of addressin each other when he was in the flesh.

"Air you in the show bizniz, William," sed I.

He sed he was. He sed he & John Bunyan was

travelin with a side show in connection with Shakspere, Jonson & Co.'s Circus. He sed old Bun (meanin Mr. Bunyan,) stired up the animils & ground the organ while he tended door. Occashunally Mr. Bunyan sung a comic song. The Circus was doin middlin well. Bill Shakspeer had made a grate hit with old Bob Ridley, and Ben Jonson was delitin the peple with his trooly grate ax of hossmanship without saddul or bridal. Thay was rehersin Dixey's Land & expected it would knock the peple.

Sez I, "William, my luvly frend, can you pay me that 13 dollars you owe me?" He sed no with one of the most tremenjis knox I ever experiunsed.

The Sircle sed he had gone. "Air you gone, William?" I axed. "Rayther," he replide, and I knowd it was no use to pursoo the subjeck furder.

I then called fur my farther.

How's things, daddy?"

' Middlin, my son, middlin."

"Ain't you proud of your orfurn boy?"

"Scacely."

"Why not, my parient?"

"Becawz you hav gone to writin for the noospapers, my son. Bimeby you'll lose all your character for trooth and verrasserty. When I helpt you into the show biznis I told you to dignerfy that there profeshun. Litteratoor is low."

He also statid that he was doin middlin well in the peanut biznis & liked it putty well, tho' the climit was rather warm.

When the Sircle stopt thay axed me what I thawt of it.

Sez I, "my frends I've bin into the show biznis now goin on 23 years. Theres a artikil in the Constitooshun of the United States which sez in effeck that everybody may think just as he darn pleazes, & them is my sentiments to a hare. You dowtlis beleeve this Sperret doctrin while I think it is a little mixt. Just so soon as a man becums a reglar out & out Sperret rapper he leeves orf workin, lets his hare grow all over his fase & commensis spungin his livin out of other peple. He eats all the dickshunaries he can find & goze round chock full of big words, scarein the wimmin folks & little children & destroyin the piece of mind of evry famerlee he enters. He don't do nobody no good & is a cuss to society & a pirit on honest peple's corn beef barrils. Admittin all you say abowt the doctrin to be troo, I must say the reglar perfessional Sperrit rappers — them as makes a biznis on it air — abowt the most ornery set of cusses I ever enkountered in my life. So sayin I put on my surtoot and went home.

Respectably Yures,

ARTEMUS WARD.

"Don't Spear me agin, if you please." [*See Page* 50.]

ON THE WING.

Gents of the Editoral Corpse;—

Since I last rit you I've met with immense success a showin my show in varis places, particly at Detroit. I put up at Mr. Russel's tavern, a very good tavern too, but I am sorry to inform you that the clerks tried to cum a Gouge Game on me. I brandished my new sixteen dollar huntin-cased watch round considerable, & as I was drest in my store clothes & had a lot of sweet-scented wagon-grease on my hair, I am free to confess that I thought I lookt putty gay. It never once struck me that I lookt green. But up steps a clerk & axes me hadn't I better put my watch in the Safe. "Sir," sez I, "that watch cost sixteen dollars! Yes Sir, every dollar of it! You can't cum it over me, my boy! Not at all, Sir." I know'd what the clerk wanted. He wanted that watch himself. He wanted to make believe as tho he lockt it up in the safe, then he would set the house a fire and pretend as tho the watch was destroyed with the other property! But he caught a Tomarter when he got hold of me. From Detroit I go West'ard hoe. On the cars was a he-lookin female, with a green-cotton umbreller in one hand and a handful of Reform tracks the other. She sed every woman should have a Spear. Them as didn't demand their Spears, didn't know what was good for them. "What is my Spear?" she axed, addressin the people in the cars. "Is it to stay at home & darn stockins & be the ser-*lave* of a domineerin man? Or is it my Spear to vote & speak & show myself the ekal of man? Is there a sister in these keers that has her proper Spear?" Sayin which the eccentric female whirled her umbreller round several times, & finally jabbed me in the weskit with it.

'I hav no objecshuns to your goin into the Spear bizness," sez I, "but you'll please remember I ain't a pickeril. Don't Spear me agin, if you please." She sot down.

At Ann Arbor, bein seized with a sudden faintness, I called for a drop of suthin to drink. As I was stirrin the beverage up, a pale-faced man in gold spectacles laid his hand upon my shoulder, & sed, "Look not upon the wine when it is red!"

Sez I, "this ain't wine. This is Old Rye."

"*It stingeth like a Adder and biteth like a Sarpent!*" sed the man.

"I guess not," sed I, "when you put sugar into it. That's the way I allers take mine."

"Have you sons grown up, Sir?" the man axed.

"Wall," I replide, as I put myself outside my beverage, "my son Artemus junior is goin on 18."

"Ain't you afraid if you set this example b4 him he'll cum to a bad end?"

"He's cum to a waxed end already. He's learnin the shoe makin bizness," I replide. "I guess we can both on us git along without your assistance, Sir," I observed, as he was about to open his mouth agin.

"This is a cold world!" sed the man.

"That's so. But you'll get into a warmer one

by and by if you don't mind your own bizness better." I was a little riled at the feller, because I never take anythin only when I'm onwell. I arterwards learned he was a temperance lecturer, and if he can injuce men to stop settin their inards on fire with the frightful licker which is retailed round the country, I shall hartily rejoice. Better give men Prusick Assid to onct, than to pizen 'em to deth by degrees.

At Albion I met with overwhelmin success. The celebrated Albion Female Semenary is located here, & there air over 300 young ladies in the Institushun, pretty enough to eat without seasonin or sass. The young ladies was very kind to me, volunteerin to pin my handbills onto the backs of their dresses. It was a surblime site to see over 300 young ladies goin round with a advertisement of A. Ward's onparaleld show, conspickusly posted onto their dresses.

They've got a Panick up this way and refooze to take Western money. It never was worth much, and when western men, who know what it is, re fooze to take their own money it is about time other folks stopt handlin it. Banks are bustin every day. goin up higher nor any balloon of which we hav any record. These western bankers air a sweet & luvly set of men. I wish I owned as good a house as some of 'em would break into!

Virtoo is its own reward.

A. WARD

THE OCTOROON.

It is with no ordernary feelins of Shagrin & indignashun that I rite you these here lines. Sum of the hiest and most purest feelins whitch actooate the humin hart has bin trampt onto. The Amerycan flag has bin outrajed. Ive bin nussin a Adder in my Boozum. The fax in the kase is these here :

A few weeks ago I left Baldinsville to go to N. Y. fur to git out my flamin yeller hanbills fur the Summer kampane, & as I was peroosin a noospaper on the kars a middel aged man in speckterkuls kum & sot down beside onto me. He was drest in black close & was appeerently as fine a man as ever was.

"A fine day Sir," he did unto me strateway say.

"Middlin," sez I, not wishin to kommit myself, tho he peered to be as fine a man as there was in the wurld — It is a middlin fine day Square," I obsarved.

Sez he, "How fares the Ship of State in yure regine of country?"

Sez I, "We don't hav no ships in our State — the kanawl is our best holt."

He pawsed a minit and then sed, "Air yu aware, Sir that the krisis is with us?"

"No," sez I, getting up and lookin under the seet, "whare is she?"

"It's hear — it's everywhares," he sed.

Sez I, "Why how you tawk!" and I gut up agin & lookt all round. "I must say my fren," I continnered, as I resoomed my seet, "that I kan't see nothin of no krisis myself." I felt sumwhat alarmed, & arose & in a stentowrian voice obsarved that if any lady or gentleman in that there kar had a krisis consealed abowt their persons they'd better projuce it to onct or suffer the konsequences. Several individoouls snickered rite out, while a putty little damsell rite behind me in a pinc gown made the observashun, "He, he."

"Sit down, my fren," sed the man in black close, "yu miskomprehend me. I meen that the perlittercal ellermunts are orecast with black klouds, 4boden a friteful storm."

"Wall," replide I, "in regard to perlittercal ellerfunts I don't know as how but what they is as good as enny other kind of ellerfunts. But I maik bold to say thay is all a ornery set & unpleasant to hav round. They air powerful hevy eaters & take up a right smart chans of room, & besides thay air as ugly and revenjeful as a Cussca-roarus Injun, with 13 inches of corn whisky in his stummick." The man in black close seemed to be as fine a man as ever was in the world. He smilt & sed praps I was rite, tho it was ellermunts instid of ellerfunts that he was alludin to, & axed me what was my prinserpuls?

"I haint gut enny," sed I — "not a prinserpul. Ime in the show biznis." The man in black close, I will hear obsarve, seemed to be as fine a man as ever was in the world.

'But," sez he, "you hav feelins into yon? You

cimpathize with the misfortunit, the loly & the hart-sick, don't you?" He bust into teers and axed me ef I saw that yung lady in the seet out yender, pintin to as slick a lookin gal as I ever seed.

Sed I, "2 be shure I see her — is she mutch sick?" The man in black close was appeerently as fine a man as ever was in the world ennywhares.

"Draw closter to me," sed the man in black close. "Let me git my mowth fernenst yure ear. Hush — SHESE A OCTOROON!"

"No!" sez I, gittin up in a exsited manner, "yu don't say so! How long has she bin in that way?"

"Frum her arliest infuncy," sed he.

"Wall, whot upon arth duz she doo it fur?" I inquired.

"She kan't help it," sed the man in black close "It's the brand of Kane."

"Wall, she'd better stop drinkin Kane's brandy," I replide.

"I sed the brand of Kane was upon her — not brandy, my fren. Yure very obtoose."

I was konsiderbul riled at this. Sez I, "My gentle Sir Ime a nonresistanter as a ginral thing, & don't want to git up no rows with nobuddy, but I kin nevertheles kave in enny man's hed that calls me a obtoos," with whitch remarks I kommenst fur to pull orf my extry garmints. "Cum on," sez I — "Time! hear's the Beniki Boy fur ye!" & I darnced round like a poppit. He riz up in his seet & axed my pardin — sed it was all a mistake — that I was a good man, etsettery, & sow 4th, & we fixt it all up pleasant. I must say the man in black close seamed to be as fine a man as ever lived in the wurld. He sed a Octoroon was the 8th of a negrow. He likewise statid that the female he was travelin with was formurly a slave in Mississippy; that she'd purchist her freedim & now wantid to purchiss the freedim of her poor old muther, who (the man in black close obsarved) was between 87 years of age & had to do all the cookin & washin for 25 hired men, whitch it was rapidly breakin down her konstitushun. He sed he knowed the minit he gazed onto my klassic & beneverlunt fase that I'd donate librully & axed me to go over & see her, which I accordinly did. I sot down beside her and sed "yure Sarvant, Marm! How do yer git along?"

She bust in 2 teers & said, "O Sur, I'm so retchid — I'm a poor unfortunit Octoroon."

"So I larn. Yure rather more Roon than Octo, I take it," sed I, fur I never seed a puttier gal in the hull endoorin time of my life. She had on a More Antic Barsk & a Poplin Nubier with Berage trimmins onto it, while her Ise & kurls was enuff to make a man jump into a mill pond without biddin his relashuns good by. I pittid the Octoroon from the inmost recusses of my hart & hawled out 50 dollers ker slap, & told her to buy her old muther as soon as posserbul. Sez she "kine sir mutch thanks." She then lade her hed over onto my showlder & sed I was "old rats." I was astonished to heer this obsarvation, which I knowd was never used in refined society & I perlitely but emfattercly shovd her hed away.

Sez I "Marm, I'm trooly sirprized."

Sez she, "git out. Yure the nicist old man Ive seen yit. Give us anuther 50!" Had a seleck assortment of the most tremenjious thunderbolts descended down onto me I couldn't hav bin more takin aback. I jumpt up, but she ceased my coat tales & in a wild voise cride, "No, Ile never desart you—let us fli together to a furrin shoor!"

Sez I, "not mutch we wont," and I made a powerful effort to get awa from her. "This is plade out," I sed, whereupon she jerkt me back into the seet. "Leggo my coat, you scandaluss female," I roared, when she set up the most unarthly yellin and hollerin you ever heerd. The passinjers & the gentlemunly konducter rusht to the spot, & I don't think I ever experiunsed sich a rumpus in the hull coarse of my natral dase. The man in black close rusht up to me & sed "How dair yu insult my neece, you horey heded vagabone! You base exhibbiter of low wax figgers — yu woolf in sheep's close," & sow 4th.

I was konfoozed. I was a loonytick fur the time bein, and cffered $5 reward to enny gentleman of good morrul carracter who wood tell me whot my name was & what town I livd into. The konductor kum to me & sed the insultid parties wood settle for $50, which I immejitly hawled out, & agane implored sumbuddy to state whare I was prinsipully, & if I shood be thare a grate while myself ef things went on as they'd bin goin fur sum time back. I then axed if there was enny more Octoroons present, "becawz," sez I, "ef there is, let um cum along, fur Ime in the Octoroon bizniss." I then threw my specterculs out of the winder, smasht my hat wildly down over my Ise, larfed highsterically & fell under a seet. I lay there sum time & fell asleep. I dreamt Mrs. Ward & the twins had bin carrid orf by Ryenosserhosses & that Baldinsville had bin captered by a army of Octoroons. When I awoked the lamps was a burnin dimly. Sum of the passinjers was a snorein like pawpusses & the little damsell in the pinc gown was a singin "Oft in the Silly nite." The onprinsipuld Octoroon & the miserbul man in black close was gone, & all of a suddent it flasht ore my brane that I'de bin swindild.

EXPERIENCE AS AN EDITOR.

In the Ortum of 18— my frend, the editor of the Baldinsville Bugle, was obleged to leave perfeshernal dooties & go & dig his taters, & he axed me to edit for him doorin his absence. Accordinly I ground up his Shears and commenced. It didn't take me a grate while to slash out copy enuff from the xchanges for one issoo, and I thawt I'd ride up to the next town on a little Jaunt, to rest my Branes which had bin severely rackt by my mental efforts. (This is sorter Ironical.) So I went over to the Rale Rood offiss and axed the Sooprintendent for a pars.

"*You* a editer?" he axed, evijently on the pint of snickerin.

"Yes Sir," sez I, "don't I look poor enuff?"

"Just about," sed he, "but our Road can't pars you."

" Can't, hay ? "

" No Sir — it can't."

" Becauz," sez I, lookin him full in the face with a Eagle eye *" it goes so darned slow it can't pars anybody!"* Methinks I had him thar. It's the slowest Rale Road in the West. With a mortifi'ed air, he told me to git out of his offiss. I pittid him and went.

OBERLIN.

About two years ago I arrove in Oberlin, Ohio. Oberlin is whare the celebrated college is. In fack, Oberlin *is* the college, everything else in that air vicinity resolvin around excloosivly for the benefit of that institution. It is a very good college, too, & a grate many wurthy yung men go there annooally to git intelleck into 'em. But its my onbiassed 'pinion that they go it rather too strong on Ethiopians at Oberlin. But that's nun of my bizness. I'm into the Show bizniss. Yit as a faithful historan I must menshun the fack that on rainy dase white peple can't find their way threw the streets without the gas is lit, there bein such a numerosity of cullerd pussons in the town.

As I was sayin, I arroved at Oberlin, and called on Perfesser Peck for the purpuss of skewerin Kolonial Hall to exhibit my wax works and beests of

Pray into. Kolonial Hall is in the college and is used by the stujents to speak peaces and read essays into.

Sez Perfesser Peck, "Mister Ward, I don't know 'bout this bizniss. What are your sentiments?"

Sez I, "I hain't got any."

"Good God!" cried the Perfesser, "did I understan you to say you hav no sentiments?"

"Nary a sentiment!" sez I.

"Mister Ward, don't your blud bile at the thawt that three million and a half of your culled brethren air a clankin their chains in the South?"

Sez I, "not a bile! Let 'em clank!"

He was about to continner his flowry speech when I put a stopper on him. Sez I, "Perfesser Peck, A. Ward is my name & Ameriky is my nashun; I'm allers the same, tho' humble is my station, and I've bin in the show bizniss goin on 22 years. The pint is, can I hav your Hall by payin a fair price? You air full of sentiments. That's your lay, while I'm a exhibiter of startlin curiosities. What d'ye say?"

"Mister Ward, you air endowed with a hily practical mind, and while I deeply regret that you air devoid of sentiments, I'll let you hav the hall provided your exhibition is of a moral & elevatin nater."

Sez I, "Tain't nothin shorter."

So I opened in Kolonial Hall, which was crowded every nite with stujents, &c. Pèrfesser Finny gazed for hours at my Kangaroo, but when that sagashus but onprincipled little cuss set up one of his onarthly yellins and I proceeded to hosswhip him, the Perfesser objected. "Suffer not your angry pashuns to rise up at the poor annimil's little excentrissities," said the Perfesser.

"Do you call such conduck as *those* a little excentrissity?" I axed.

"I do," sed he, sayin which he walked up to the cage and sez he, "let's try moral swashun upon the poor creeter." So he put his hand upon the Kangeroo's hed and sed, "poor little feller — poor little feller — your master is very crooil, isn't he, my untootered frend," when the Kangaroo, with a terrific yell, grabd the Perfesser by the hand and cum very near chawin it orf. It was amoozin to see the Perfesser jump up and scream with pane. Sez I, "that's one of the poor little feller's excentrissities!"

Sez he, "Mister Ward, that's a dangerous quadruped. He's totally depraved. I will retire and do my lasserated hand up in a rag, and meanwhile I request you to meat out summery and severe punishment to the vishus beest. I hosswhipt the little cuss for upwards 15 minutes. Guess I licked sum of his excentrissity out of him.

Oberlin is a grate plase. The College opens with a prayer and then the New York Tribune is read. A kolleckshun is then taken up to buy overkoats with red horn buttons onto them for the indignant cullured people of Kanady. I have to contribit librally two the glowrius work, as they kawl it hear. I'm kompelled by the Fackulty to reserve front seets in my show for the cullered peple. At the Boardin House the cullered peple sit at the first table. What they leeve is maid into hash for the white peple. As I don't like the idee of eatin my vittles with Ethiopians, I sit at the seckind table, and the konsequence is I've devowered so much hash that my inards is in a hily mixt up condishun. Fish bones hav maid their appearance all over my boddy and pertater peelins air a springin up through my hair. Howsever I don't mind it. I'm gittin along well in a pecunery pint of view. The College has konfired upon me the honery title of T. K., of which I'm suffishuntly prowd.

THE SHOWMAN'S COURTSHIP.

Thare was many affectin ties which made me hanker arter Betsy Jane. Her father's farm jined our'n; their cows and our'n squencht their thurst at the same spring; our old mares both had stars in their forrerds; the measles broke out in both famerlies at nearly the same period; our parients (Betsy's and mine) slept reglarly every Sunday in the same meetin house, and the nabers used to obsarve, "How thick the Wards and Peasleys air!" It was a surblime site, in the Spring of the year, to see our sevral mothers (Betsy's and mine) with their gowns pin'd up so thay could'nt sile 'em, affecshunitly Bilin sope together & aboozin the nabers.

Altho I hankerd intensly arter the objeck of my

affecshuns, I darsunt tell her of the fires which was rajin in my manly Buzzum. I'd try to do it but my tung would kerwollup up agin the roof of my mowth & stick thar, like deth to a deseast Afrikan or a country postmaster to his offiss, while my hart whanged agin my ribs like a old fashioned wheat Flale agin a barn floor.

T'was a carm still nite in Joon. All nater was husht and nary zeffer disturbed the sereen silens. I sot with Betsy Jane on the fense of her farther's pastur. We'd bin rompin threw the woods, kullin flours & drivin the woodchuck from his Nativ Lair (so to speak) with long sticks. Wall we sot thar on the fense, a swingin our feet two and fro, blushin as red as the Baldinsville skool house when it was fust painted, and lookin very simple, I make no doubt. My left arm was ockepied in ballunsin myself on the fense, while my rite was woundid luvinly round her waste.

I cleared my throat and tremblinly sed, "Betsy, you're a Gazelle."

I thought that air was putty fine. I waitid to

see what effeck it would hav upon her. It evidently didn't fetch her, for she up and sed,

"You're a sheep!"

Sez I, "Betsy, I think very muchly of you."

"I don't b'leeve a word you say — so there now cum!" with which obsarvashun she hitched away from me.

"I wish thar was winders to my Sole," sed I, "so that you could see some of my feelins. There's fire enuff in here," sed I, strikin my buzzum with my fist, "to bile all the corn beef and turnips in the naberhood. Versoovius and the Critter ain't a circumstans!"

She bowd her hed down and commenst chawin the strings to her sun bonnet.

"Ar, could you know the sleeplis nites I worry threw with on your account, how vittles has seized to be attractiv to me & how my lims has shrunk up, you would'nt dowt me. Gase on this wastin form and these 'ere sunken cheeks" —

I should have continnered on in this strane probly for sum time, but unfortnitly I lost my ballunse and fell over into the pastur ker smash, tearin my close and severly damagin myself ginerally.

Betsy Jane sprung to my assistance in dubble quick time and dragged me 4th. Then drawin herself up to her full hite she sed:

"I won't listen to your noncents no longer. Jes say rite strate out what you're drivin at. If you mean gettin hitched, I'M IN!"

I considered that air enuff for all practicul purpusses, and we proceeded immejitly to the parson's, & was made 1 that very nite.

(Notiss to the Printer: Put some stars here.)

* * * * * * *

I've parst threw many tryin ordeels sins then, but Betsy Jane has bin troo as steel. By attendin strickly to bizniss I've amarsed a handsum Pittance. No man on this foot-stool can rise & git up & say I ever knowinly injered no man or wimmin folks, while all agree that my Show is ekalled by few and exceld by none, embracin as it does a wonderful colleckshun of livin wild Beests of Pray, snaix in grate profushun, a endliss variety of life-size wax figgers, & the only traned kangaroo in Ameriky — the most amoozin little cuss ever introjuced to a discriminatin public.

THE CRISIS.

[This Oration was delivered before the commencement of the war.]

On returnin to my humsted in Baldinsville, Injianny, resuntly, my feller sitterzens extended a invite for me to norate to 'em on the Krysis. I excepted & on larst Toosday nite I peared be4 a C of upturned faces in the Red Skool House. I spoke nearly as follers:

Baldinsvillins: Hearto4, as I hav numerously obsarved, I have abstrained from having any sentimunts or principles, my pollertics, like my religion, bein of a exceedin accommodatin character. But the fack can't be no longer disgised that a Krysis is onto us, & I feel it's my dooty to accept your invite for one consecutive nite only. I spose the inflammertory individooals who assisted in projucing this Krysis know what good she will do, but I ain't

"SHALL THE STAR SPANGLED BANNER BE CUT UP INTO DISH CLOTHS?" [*See Page* 80.]

'shamed to state that I don't, scacely. But the Krysis is hear. She's bin hear for sevral weeks, & Goodness nose how long she'll stay. But I venter to assert that she's rippin things. She's knockt trade into a cockt up hat and chaned Bizness of all kinds tighter nor I ever chaned any of my livin wild Beests. Alow me to hear dygress & stait that my Beests at presnt is as harmless as the new-born Babe. Ladys & gentlemen needn't hav no fears on that pint. To resoom — Altho I can't exactly see what good this Krysis can do, I can very quick say what the origernal cawz of her is. The origernal cawz is Our Afrikan Brother. I was into BARNIM'S Moozeum down to New York the other day & saw that exsentric Etheopian, the What Is It. Sez I, "Mister What Is It, you folks air raisin thunder with this grate country. You're gettin to be ruther more numeris than interestin. It is a pity you coodent go orf sumwhares by yourselves, & be a nation of What Is Its, tho' if you'll excoose me, I shooden't care about marryin among you. No dowt you're exceedin charmin to hum, but your stile of luvliness isn't adapted to this cold climit. He larfed into my face, which rather Riled me, as I had been perfeckly virtoous and respectable in my observashuns. So sez I, turnin a leetle red in the face I spect, "Do you hav the unblushin impoodents to say you folks haven't raised a big mess of thunder in this brite land, Mister What Is It?" He larfed agin, wusser nor be4, whareupon I up and sez, "Go home, Sir, to Afriky's burnin shores & taik all the other What Is Its along with you. Don't think we can't spair your interestin picters. You What Is Its air on the pint of smashin up the gratest Guv'ment ever erected by man, & you actooally hav the owdassity to larf about it. Go home, you low cuss!"

I was workt up to a high pitch, & I proceeded to a Restorator & cooled orf with some little fishes biled in ile — I b'leeve thay call 'em sardeens.

Feller Sitterzuns, the Afrikan may be Our Brother. Sevral hily respectyble gentlemen, and sum talentid females tell us so, & fur argyment's sake I mite be injooced to grant it, tho' I don't beleeve it myself. But the Afrikan isn't our sister &

our wife & our uncle. He isn't sevral of our brothers & all our fust wife's relashuns. He isn't our grandfather, and our grate grandfather,and our Aunt in the country. Scacely. & yit numeris persons would have us think so. It's troo he runs Congress & sevral other public grosserys, but then he ain't everybody & everybody else likewise. [Notiss to bizness man of VANITY FAIR: Extry charg fur this larst remark. It's a goak.—A. W.]

But we've got the Afrikan, or ruther he's got us, & now what air we going to do about it? He's a orful noosanse. Praps he isn't to blame fur it. Praps he was creatid fur sum wise purpuss, like the measles and New Englan Rum, but it's mity hard to see it. At any rate he's no good here, & as I statid to Mister What Is It, it's a pity he cooden't go orf sumwhares quietly by hisself, whare he cood wear red weskits & speckled neckties, & gratterfy his ambishun in varis interestin wase, without havin a eternal fuss kickt up about him.

Praps I'm bearin down too hard upon Cuffy. Cum to think on it, I am. He wooden't be sich a infernal noosanse if white peple would let him alone. He mite indeed be interestin. And now I think of it, why can't the white peple let him alone. What's the good of continnerly stirrin him up with a ten-foot pole? He isn't the sweetest kind of Perfoomery when in a natral stait.

Feller Sitterzens, the Union's in danger. The black devil Disunion is trooly here, starein us all squarely in the face! We must drive him back. Shall we make a 2nd Mexico of ourselves? Shall we sell our birthrite for a mess of potash? Shall one brother put the knife to the throat of anuther brother? Shall we mix our whisky with each others' blud? Shall the star spangled Banner be cut up into dishcloths? Standin here in this here Skoolhouse, upon my nativ shore so to speak, I anser — Nary!

Oh you fellers who air raisin this row, & who in the fust place startid it, I'm 'shamed of you. The Showman blushes for you, from his boots to the topmost hair upon his wenerable hed.

Feller Sitterzens, I am in the Sheer & Yeller

leaf. I shall peg out 1 of these dase. But while I do stop here I shall stay in the Union. I know not what the supervizers of Baldinsville may conclude to do, but for one, I shall stand by the Stars & Stripes. Under no circumstances whatsomever will I sesesh. Let every Stait in the Union sesesh & let Palmetter flags flote thicker nor shirts on Square Baxter's close line, still will I stick to the good old flag. The country may go to the devil, but I won't! And next Summer when I start out on my campane with my Show, wharever I pitch my little tent, you shall see floatin prowdly from the center pole thereof the Amerikan Flag, with nary a star wiped out, nary a stripe less, but the same old flag that has allers flotid thar! & the price of admishun will be the same it allers was — 15 cents, children half price.

Feller Sitterzens, I am dun. Accordinly I squatted.

WAX FIGURES VS. SHAKSPEARE.

ONTO THE WING —— 1859.

MR. EDITOR ;

I take my Pen in hand to inform yu that I'm in good helth and trust these few lines will find yu injoyin the same blessins. I wood also state that I'm now on the summir kampane. As the Poit sez —

ime erflote, ime erflote
On the Swift rollin tied
An the Rovir is free.

Bizness is scacely middlin, but Sirs I manige to pay for my foode and raiment puncktooally and without no grumblin. The barked arrers of slandur has bin leviled at the undersined moren onct sins heze bin into the show bizness, but I make bold to say no man on this footstule kan troothfully say I ever ronged him or eny of his folks. I'm travelin with a tent, which is better nor hirin hauls. My show konsists of a serious of wax works, snakes, a paneramy kalled a Grand Movin Diarea of the War in the Crymear, komic songs and the Cangeroo, which larst little cuss continners to konduct hisself in the most outrajus stile. I started out with the idear of makin my show a grate Moral Entertainment, but I'm kompeled to sware so much at that air infurnal Kangeroo that I'm frade this desine will be flustratid to some extent. And while speakin of morrality, remines me that sum folks turn up their nosis at shows like mine, sayin they is low and not fit to be patrernized by peple of high degree. Sirs, I manetane that this is infernul nonsense. I manetane that wax figgers is more elevatin than awl the plays ever wroten. Take Shakespeer for instunse. Peple think heze grate things, but I kontend heze quite the reverse to the konrtary. What sort of sense is thare to King Leer who goze round cussin his darters, chawin hay and throin straw at folks, and larfin like a silly old koot and makin a ass of hisself ginerally? Thare's Mrs. Mackbeth — sheze a nise kind of woomon to have round aint she, a puttin old Mack, her husband, up to slayin Dunkan with a cheeze knife, while heze payin a frendly visit to their house. O its hily morral, I spoze, when she larfs wildly and sez, "gin me the daggurs — Ile let his bowels out," or wurds to that effeck — I say, this is awl strickly propper I spoze? That Jack Fawlstarf is likewise a immoral old cuss, take him how ye may, and Hamlick is as crazy as a loon. Thare's Richurd the Three peple think heze grate things, but I look upon him in the lite of a monkster. He kills everybody he takes a noshun to in kold blud, and then goze to sleep in his tent. Bimeby he wakes up and yells for a hoss so he kan go orf and kill sum more peple. If he isent a fit spesserman for the gallers then I shood like to know whare you find um. Thare's Iargo who is more crnery nor pizun. See how shamful he treated that hily respecterble injun gentlemun, Mister Otheller, makin him for to beleeve his wife was two thick with Casheo. Obsarve how Iargo got Casheo drunk as a biled owl on corn whisky in order to karry out his sneekin desines. See how he wurks Mister Otheller's feelins up so that he goze and makes poor Desdemony swaller a piller which cawses her deth. But I must stop. At sum futur time I shall continner my remarks on the dramer in which I shall show the varst supeeriority of wax figgers and snakes over theater plays, in a in terlectooal pint of view.

Very Respectively yures,

A. WARD, T. K.

AMONG THE FREE LOVERS.*

Some years ago I pitched my tent and onfurled my banner to the breeze, in Berlin Hites, Ohio. I had hearn that Berlin Hites was ockepied by a extensive seck called Free Lovers, who beleeved in affinertys and sich, goin back on their domestic ties without no hesitation whatsomever. They was likewise spirit rappers and high presher reformers on gineral principles. If I can improve these 'ere misgided peple by showin them my onparalleld show at the usual low price of admitants, methunk, I shall not hav lived in vane! But bitterly did I cuss the day I ever sot foot in the retchid place. I sot up my tent in a field near the Love Cure, as they called it, and bimeby the free lovers begun for

* Some queer people, calling themselves "Free Lovers," and possessing very original ideas about life and morality, established themselves at Berlin Heights, in Ohio, a few years since. Public opinion was resistlessly against them, however, and the association was soon disbanded.

to congregate around the door. A ornreer set I have never sawn. The men's faces was all covered with hare and they lookt half-starved to deth. They didn't wear no weskuts for the purpuss (as they sed) of allowin the free air of hevun to blow onto their boozums. Their pockets was filled with tracks and pamplits and they was bare-footed. They sed the Postles didn't wear boots, & why should they? That was their stile of argyment. The wimin was wuss than the men. They wore trowsis, short gownds, straw hats with green ribbins, and all carried bloo cotton umbrellers.

Presently a perfeckly orful lookin female presented herself at the door. Her gownd was skanderlusly short and her trowsis was shameful to behold.

She eyed me over very sharp, and then startin back she sed, in a wild voice:

"Ah, can it be?"

"Which?" sed I.

"Yes, 'tis troo, O 'tis troo!"

"15 cents, marm," I anserd.

She bust out a cryin & sed:

"And so I hav found you at larst — at larst, O at larst!"

"Yes," I anserd, "you have found me at larst, and you would have found me at fust, if you had cum sooner."

She grabd me vilently by the coat collar, and brandishin her umbreller wildly round, exclaimed:

"Air you a man?"

Sez I, "I think I air, but if you doubt it, you can address Mrs. A. Ward, Baldinsville, Injianny, postage pade, & she will probly giv you the desired informashun."

"Then thou ist what the cold world calls marrid?"

"Madam, I istest!"

The exsentric female then clutched me franticly by the arm and hollerd:

"You air mine, O you air mine!"

"Scacely," I sed, endeverin to git loose from her. But she clung to me and sed:

"You air my Affinerty!"

"What upon arth is that?" I shouted.

"Dost thou not know?"

"No, I dostent!"

"Listin man, & I'll tell ye!" sed the strange female; "for years I hav yearned for thee. I knowd thou wast in the world, sumwhares, tho I didn't know whare. My hart sed he would cum and I took courage. He *has* cum — he's here — you air him — you air my Affinerty! O 'tis too mutch! too mutch!" and she sobbed agin.

"Yes," I anserd, "I think it is a darn site too mutch!"

"Hast thou not yearned for me?" she yelled, ringin her hands like a female play acter.

"Not a yearn!" I bellerd at the top of my voice, throwin her away from me.

The free lovers who was standin round obsarvin the scene commenst for to holler "shame!" "beast," etsettery, etsettery.

I was very mutch riled, and fortifyin myself with a spare tent stake, I addrest them as follers: "You pussylanermus critters, go way from me and take this retchid woman with you. I'm a law-abidin man, and bleeve in good, old-fashioned institutions. I am marrid & my orfsprings resemble me, if I am a showman! I think your Affinity bizniss is cussed noncents, besides bein outrajusly wicked. Why don't you behave desunt like other folks? Go to work and earn a honist livin and not stay round here in this lazy, shiftless way, pizenin the moral atmosphere with your pestifrous idees! You wimin folks go back to your lawful husbands if you've got any, and take orf them skanderlous gownds and trowsis, and dress respectful like other wimin. You men folks, cut orf them pirattercal whiskers, burn up them infurnel pamplits, put sum weskuts on, go to work choppin wood, splittin fence rales, or tillin the sile. I pored 4th my indignashun in this way till I got out of breth, when I stopt. I shant go to Berlin Hites agin, not if I live to be as old as Methooseler.

SCANDALOUS DOINGS AT PITTSBURGH.

Hear in the Buzzum of my famerly I am enjoyin myself, at peas with awl mankind and the wimmin folks likewize. I go down to the village ockashunly and take a little old Rye fur the stummuck's sake, but I avoyd spiritus lickers as a ginral thing. No man evir seen me intossikated but onct, and that air happind in Pittsburg. A parsel of ornery cusses in that luvly sity bustid inter the hawl durin the nite and aboosed my wax works shaimful. I didnt obsarve the outrajus transacshuns ontil the next evening when the peple begun for to kongregate. Suddinly thay kommensed fur to larf and holler in a boysterious stile. Sez I good peple wha'ts up? Sez thay them's grate wax wurks, isn't they, old man. I immejitly looked up ter whare the wax works was and my blud biles as I think of the site which then met my Gase. I hope two be dodrabbertid if them afoursed raskals hadent gone and put a old kaved in hat onter George Washington's hed and shuved a short black klay pipe inter his mouth. His noze thay had painted red and his trowsis legs thay had shuvd inside his butes. My wax figger of Napoleon Boneypart was likewise mawltreatid. His sword wus danglin tween his legs, his cockd hat was drawn klean down over his ize,and he was plased in a stoopin posishun lookin zactly as tho he was as drunk as a biled owl. Ginral Tayler was a standin on his hed and Wingfield Skott's koat tales ware pind over his hed and his trowsis ware kompleetly torn orf frum hisself. My wax works representin the Lord's Last Supper was likewise aboozed. Three of the Postles ware under the table and two of um had on old tarpawlin hats and raggid pee jackits and ware smokin pipes. Judus Iskarriot had on a cocked hat and was appeerently drinkin, as a Bottle of whisky sct befour him. This ere specktercal was too much fur me. I klosed the show and then drowndid my sorrers in the flowin Bole

"Oh stay, Sir, stay!" sed a tall gawnt femail. [*Se Page* 101.]

A VISIT TO BRIGHAM YOUNG.

It is now goin on 2 (too) yeres, as I very well, remember, since I crossed the Planes for Kaliforny, the Brite land of Jold. While crossin the Planes all so bold I fell in with sum noble red men of the forest (N. B. This is rote Sarcasticul. Injins is Pizin, whar ever found,) which thay Sed I was their Brother, & wantid for to smoke the Calomel of Peace with me. Thay then stole my jerkt beef, blankits, etsettery, skalpt my orgin grinder & scooted with a Wild Hoop. Durin the Cheaf's techin speech he sed he shood meet me in the Happy Huntin Grounds. If he duz thare will be a fite. But enuff of this ere. ***Reven Noose Muttons***, as our skoolmaster, who has got Talent into him, cussycally obsarve.

I arrove at Salt Lake in doo time. At Camp Scott there was a lot of U. S. sojers, hosstensibly sent out thare to smash the mormons but really tc eat Salt vittles & play poker & other beautiful but sumwhat onsartin games. I got acquainted with sum of the officers. Thay lookt putty scrumpshus in their Bloo coats with brass buttings onto um & ware very talented drinkers, but so fur as fitin is consarned I'd willingly put my wax figgers agin the hull party.

My desire was to exhibit my grate show in Salt Lake City, so I called on Brigham Yung, the grate mogull amung the mormins, and axed his permishun to pitch my tent and onfurl my banner to the jentle breezis. He lookt at me in a austeer manner for a few minits, and sed:

"Do you bleeve in Solomon, Saint Paul, the immaculateness of the Mormin Church and the Latter-day Revelashuns?"

Sez I, "I'm on it!" I make it a pint to git along plesunt, tho I didn't know what under the Son the old feller was drivin at. He sed I mite show.

"You air a marrid man, Mister Yung, I bleeve?" sez I, preparin to rite him sum free parsis.

"I hev eighty wives, Mister Ward. I sertinly am marrid."

"How do you like it as far as you hev got?" sed I.

He sed "middlin," and axed me wouldn't I like to see his famerly, to which I replide that I wouldn't mind minglin with the fair Seck & Barskin in the winnin smiles of his interestin wives. He accordingly tuk me to his Scareum. The house is powerful big & in a exceedin large room was his wives & children, which larst was squawkin and hollerin enuff to take the roof rite orf the house. The wimin was of all sizes and ages. Sum was pretty & sum was plane — sum was helthy and sum was on the Wayne — which is verses, tho sich was not my intentions, as I don't 'prove of puttin verses in Proze rittins, tho ef occashun requires I can Jerk a Poim ekal to any of them Atlantic Munthly fellers.

"My wives, Mister Ward," sed Yung.

"Your sarvant, marms," sed I, as I sot down in a cheer which a red-heded female brawt me.

"Besides these wives you see here, Mister Ward,'

sed Yung, "I hav eighty more in varis parts of this consecrated land which air Sealed to me."

"Which?" sez I, gittin up & starin at him.

"Sealed, Sir! sealed."

"Whare bowts?" sez I.

"I sed, Sir, that they was sealed!" He spoke in a traggerdy voice.

"Will they probly continner on in that stile to any grate extent, Sir?" I axed.

"Sir," sed he furnin as red as a biled beet, "don't you know that the rules of our Church is that I, the Profit, may hev as meny wives as I wants?"

"Jes so," I sed. "You are old pie, ain't you?"

"Them as is Sealed to me — that is to say, to be mine when I wants um — air at present my sperretooul wives," sed Mister Yung.

"Long may thay wave!" sez I, seein I shood git into a scrape ef I didn't look out.

In a privit conversashun with Brigham I learnt the follerin fax: It takes him six weeks to kiss his wives. He don't do it only onct a yere & sez it is wuss nor cleanin house. He don't pretend to know his children, thare is so many of um, tho they all know him. He sez about every child he meats call him Par, & he takes it for grantid it is so. His wives air very expensiv. Thay allers want suthin & ef he don't buy it for um thay set the house in a uproar. He sez he don't have a minit's peace. His wives fite amung theirselves so much that he has bilt a fitin room for thare speshul benefit, & when too of 'em get into a row he has em turnd loose into that place, whare the dispoot is settled accordin to the rules of the London prize ring. Sumtimes thay abooz hisself individooally. Thay hev pulled the most of his hair out at the roots & he wares meny a horrible scar upon his body, inflicted with mop-handles, broom-sticks and sich. Occashunly they git mad & scald him with bilin hot water. When he got eny waze cranky thay'd shut him up in a dark closit, previsly whippin him arter the stile of muthers when thare orfsprings git onruly. Sumtimes when he went in swimmin thay'd go to the banks of the Lake & steal all his close, thereby compellin him to sneek home by a sircootius rowt, drest in the Skanderlus stile of the Greek Slaiv. "I find that the keers of a marrid life way hevy onto me," sed the Profit, "& sumtimes I wish I'd remaned singel." I left the Profit and startid for the tavern whare I put up to. On my way I was overtuk by a lurge krowd of Mormons, which they surroundid me & statid that they were goin into the Show free.

"Wall," sez I, "ef I find a individooal who is goin round lettin folks into his show free, I'll let you know."

"We've had a Revelashun biddin us go into A. Ward's Show without payin nothin!" thay showtid.

"Yes," hollered a lot of femaile Mormonesses, ceasin me by the cote tales & swingin me round very rapid, "we're all goin in free! So sez the Revelashun!"

"What's Old Revelashun got to do with my Show?" sez I, gittin putty rily. "Tell Mister Revelashun," sed I, drawin myself up to my full hite and lookin round upon the ornery krowd with a prowd & defiant mean, "tell Mister Revelashun to mind his own bizness, subject only to the Konstitushun of the Unitid States!"

"Oh now let us in, that's a sweet man," sed several femails, puttin thare arms rownd me in luvin stile. "Becum 1 of us. Becum a Preest & hav wives Sealed to you."

"Not a Seal!" sez I, startin back in horror at the idee.

"Oh stay, Sir, stay," sed a tall, gawnt femaile, ore whoos hed 37 summirs must hev parsd, "stay, & I'll be your Jentle Gazelle."

"Not ef I know it, you won't," sez I. "Awa you skanderlus femaile, awa! Go & be a Nunnery!" That's what I sed, jes so.

"& I," sed a fat chunky femaile, who must hev wade more than too hundred lbs., "I will be your sweet gidin Star!"

Sez I, "Ile bet two dollers and a half you won't!" Whare ear I may Rome Ile still be troo 2 thee, Oh Betsy Jane! [N. B Betsy Jane is my wife's Sir naime.]

"Wiltist thou not tarry hear in the Promist Land?" sed several of the miserabil critters.

"Ile see you all essenshally cussed be 4 I wiltist!" roared I, as mad as I cood be at thare infernul non-cents. I girdid up my Lions & fled the Seen. I packt up my duds & left Salt Lake, which is a 2nd Soddum & Germorrer, inhabitid by as theavin & onprincipled a set of retchis as ever drew Breth in eny spot on the Globe.

THE CENSUS.

The Sences taker in our town bein taken sick he deppertised me to go out for him one day, and as he was too ill to giv me informashun how to perceed, I was consekently compelled to go it blind. Sittin down by the road side I drawd up the follerin list of questions which I proposed to ax the peple I visited :

Wat's your age ?

Whar was you born ?

Air yon marrid, and if so how do you like it ?

How many children hav you, and do they sufficiently resemble you as to proclood the possibility of their belongin to any of your nabers ?

Did you ever hav the measels, and if so how many ?

Hav you a twin brother several years older than yourself ?

How many parents hav you?

Do you read Watt's Hims regler?

Do you use boughten tobacker?

Wat's your fitin wate?

Air you trubeld with biles?

How does your meresham culler?

State whether you air blind, deaf, idiotic or got the heaves?

Do you know any Opry singers, and if so how much do they owe you?

What's the average of virtoo on the Ery Canawl?

If 4 barrils of Emptins pored onto a barn floor will kiver it how many plase can Dion Boureicault write in a year?

Is Beans a regler article of diet in your family?

How many chickins hav you, on foot and in the shell?

Air you aware that Injianny whisky is used in New York shootin galrys instid of pistils, and that i shoots furthest?

Was you ever at Niagry Falls?

Was you ever in the Penitentiary?

State how much pork, impendin crysis, Dutch cheeze, popler suvrinty, standard poetry, childrens' strainer's, slave code, catnip, red flannel, ancient histry, pickled tomaters, old junk, perfoomery, coal ile, liberty, hoop skirt, &c., you hav on hand?

But it didn't work. I got into a row at the fust house I stopt to, with some old maids. Disbelieven the ansers they giv in regard to their ages I endevered to open their mouths and look at their teeth, same as they do with hosses, but they floo into a vilent rage and tackled me with brooms and sich. Takin the senses requires experiunse, like any other bizniss.

AN HONEST LIVING.

I was on my way from the mines to San Francisco, with a light puss and a hevy hart. You'd scarcely hav recognized my fair form, so kiverd was I with dust. Bimeby I met Old Poodles, the allfirdist gambler in the country. He was afoot and in his shirt sleeves, and was in a wuss larther nor any race hoss I ever saw.

"Whither goist thow, sweet nimp?" sez I, in a play-actin tone.

"To the mines, Sir," he unto me did say," to the mines, *to earn an honest livin.*"

Thinks I that air aint very cool, I guess, and druv on.

THE PRESS.

I want the editers to cum to my Show free as the flours of May, but I don't want um to ride a free hoss to deth. Thare is times when Patience seizes to be virtoous. I hev "in my mind's eye, Hurrashio" (cotashun from Hamlick) sum editers in a sertin town which shall be nameless, who air Both sneakin and ornery. They cum in krowds to my Show and then axt me ten sents a lines for Puffs. I objectid to payin, but they sed ef I didn't down with the dust thay'd wipe my Show from the face of the earth! Thay sed the Press was the Arkymedian Leaver which moved the wurld. I put up to their extorshuns until thay'd bled me so I was a meer shadder, and left in disgust.

It was in a surtin town in Virginny, the Muther of Presidents & things, that I was shaimfully aboozed by a editor in human form. He set my Show up steep & kalled me the urbane & gentlemunly manajer, but when I, fur the purpuss of showin fair play all around, went to anuther offiss to git my handbills printed, what duz this pussillanermus editer do but change his toon & abooze me like a Injun. He sed my wax wurks was a humbug & called me a horey-heded itinerent vagabone. I thort at fust Ide pollish him orf ar-lar the Beneki Boy, but on reflectin that he cood pollish me much wuss in his paper, I giv it up. & I wood here take occashun to advise peple when thay run agin, as thay sumtimes will, these miserable papers, to not pay nc attenshun to um. Abuv all, don't assault a editer of this kind. It only gives him a notorosity, which is jest what he wants, & don't do you no more good than it wood to jump into enny other mud puddle. Editers are generally fine men, but there must be black sheep in every flock.

"Fair Youth, do you know whot I'd do with you if you was my sun?" [*See Page* 112.]

EDWIN FORREST AS OTHELLO.

Durin a recent visit to New York the undersined went to see Edwin Forrest. As I'm into the moral show bizness myself, I ginrally go to Barnum's moral Museum, where only moral peple air admitted, partickly on Wednesday arternoons. But this time I thot I'd go & see Ed. Ed has bin actin out on the stage for many years. There is varis 'pinions about his actin, Englishmen ginrally bleevin that he is far superior to Mister Macready; but on one pint all agree, & that is that Ed draws like a six ox team. Ed was actin at Niblo's Garding, which looks considerable more like a parster than a garding, but let that pars. I sot down in the pit, took out my spectacles & commenced peroosin the evenin's bill. The awjince was all-fired large & the boxes was full of the elitty of New York. Sevral opery glasses was leveld at me by Gothum's fairest darters. but I didn't let on as tho I noticed it, tho mebby I did take out my sixteen-dollar silver watch & brandish it round more than was necessary. But the best of us has our weaknesses & if a man has gewelry let him show it. As I was peroosin the bill a grave young man who sot near me, axed me if I'd ever seen Forrest dance the Essence of Old Virginny?" "He's immense in that," sed the young man. "He also does a fair champion jig," the young man continnerd, "but his Big Thing is the Essence of Old Virginny." Sez I, "Fair youth, do you know what I'd do with you if you was my sun?"

"No," sez he.

"Wall," sez I, "I'd appint your funeral to-morrow arternoon & the *korps should be ready!* You're too smart to live on this yearth." He didn't try any more of his capers on me. But another pussylanermuss individooul, in a red vest & patent lether boots, told me his name was Bill Astor & axed me to lend him 50 cents till early in the mornin. I told him I'd probly send it round to him before he retired to his virtoous couch, but if I didn't he might look for it next fall, as soon as I cut my corn. The Orchestry was now fiddling with all their might, & as the peple didn't understan anything about it they applaudid versifrussly. Presently, Old Ed cum out. The play was Otheller or More of Veniss. Otheller was writ by Wm. Shakspeer. The scene is laid in Veniss. Otheller was a likely man & was a ginral in the Veniss army. He eloped with Desdemony, a darter of the Hon. Mister Brabantio, who represented one of the back districks in the Veneshun legislater. Old Brabantio was as mad as thunder at this & tore round considerable, but finally cooled down, tellin Otheller, howsever, that Desdemony had come it over her Par, & that he had better look out or she'd come it over him likewise. Mr. & Mrs. Otheller git along very comfortable like for a spell. She is sweet-tempered and luvin — a nice, sensible female, never goin in for he-female conventions, green cotton umbrellers and pickled beats. Otheller is a good provider and thinks all the world of his wife. She has a lazy time of it, the hired girl doin all the cookin and washin. Desdemony, in fact, don't hav to git the water to wash her own hands with. But a low cuss named Iago, who I bleeve wants to git Otheller out of his snug government birth, now goes to work & upsets the Otheller family in the most outrajus stile. Iago falls in with a braneless youth named Roderigo & wins all his money at poker. (Iago allers played foul.) He thus got money enuff to carry out his onprincipled skeem. Mike Cassio, a Irish man, is selected as a tool by Iago. Mike was a clever feller & orficer in Otheller's army. He liked his tods too well, howsever, & they floored him, as they have many other promisin young men. Iago injuces Mike to drink with him, Iago slyly throwin his whisky over his shoulder. Mike gits as drunk as a biled owl & allows that he can lick a yard full of the Veneshun fancy before breakfast, without sweatin a hair. He meets Roderigo & proceeds for to smash him. A feller named Montano undertakes to slap Cassio, when that infatooated person runs his sword into him. That miserble man, Iago, pretents to be very sorry to see Mike conduck hisself in this way, & undertakes to smooth the thing over tc Otheller, who rushes in with a drawn sword & wants to know what's up. Iago cunninly tells his story, & Otheller tells Mike that he thinks a good deal of him but he can't train no more in his regiment. Desdemony sympathises with poor Mike & interceeds for him with Otheller. Iago makes him bleeve she does this because she thinks more of Mike than she does of hisself. Otheller swallers Iago's lyin tail & goes to makin a noosence of hisself ginrally. He worries poor Desdemony terrible by his vile insinuations & finally smothers her to deth with a piller. Mrs. Iago cums in just as Otheller has finished the fowl deed & givs him fits right & left, showin him that he has bin orfully gulled by her miserble cuss of a husband. Iago cums in, & his wife commences rakin him down also, when he stabs her. Otheller jaws him a spell & then cuts a small hole in his stummick with his sword. Iago pints to Desdemony's deth bed & goes orf with a sardonic smile onto his countenance. Otheller tells the peple that he has dun the state sum service & they know it; axes them to do as fair a thing as they can for him under the circumstances, & kills hisself with a fish-knife, which is the most sensible thing he can do. This is a breef skedule of the synopsis of the play.

Edwin Forrest is a grate acter. I thot I saw Otheller before me all the time he was actin, & when the curtin fell, I found my spectacles was still mistened with salt-water, which had run from my eyes while poor Desdemony was dyin. Betsy Jane — Betsy Jane! let us pray that our domestic bliss may never be busted up by a Iago!

Edwin Forrest makes money actin out on the stage. He gits five-hundred dollars a nite & his board & washin. I wish I had such a Forrest in my Garding!

THE SHOW BUSINESS AND POPULAR LECTURES.*

I feel that the Show Bizniss, which Ive stroven to ornyment, is bein usurpt by Poplar Lecturs, as thay air kalled, tho in my pinion thay air poplar humbugs. Individoouls, who git hard up, embark in the lecturin biznis. Thay cram theirselves with hi soundin frazis, frizzle up their hare, git trustid for a soot of black close & cum out to lectur at 50 dollers a pop. Thay aint over stockt with branes, but thay hav brass enuff to make suffishunt kittles to bile all the sope that will be required by the ensooin sixteen ginerashuns. Peple flock to heer um in krowds. The men go becawz its poplar & the wimin folks go to see what other wimin folks have on. When its over the lecturer goze & ragales his-

* It is proper to say that MR. WARD has recently found occasion to change his mind on this subject.

self with oysters and sich, while the peple say "What a charmin lectur that air was," etsettery etsettery, when 9 out of 10 of um don't have no moore idee of what the lecturer sed than my kangeroo has of the sevunth speer of hevun. Thare's moore infurmashun to be gut out of a well conductid noospaper — price 3 sents — than thare is out of ten poplar lectures at 25 or 50 dollers a pop, as the kase may be. These same peple, bare in mind stick up their nosis at moral wax figgers & sagashus beests. Thay say these things is low. Gents, it greeves my hart in my old age, when I'm in "the Sheer & yeller leef" (to cote frum my Irish frend Mister McBeth) to see that the Show biznis is pritty much plade out. howsomever I shall chance it agane in the Spring.

WOMAN'S RIGHTS.

I pitcht my tent in a small town in Injianny one day last seeson, & while I was standin at the dore takin money, a deppytashun of ladies came up & sed they wos members of the Bunkumville Female Moral Reformin & Wimin's Rite's Associashun, and thay axed me if they cood go in without payin.

"Not exactly," sez I, "but you can pay without goin in."

"Dew you know who we air?" said one of the wimin — a tall and feroshus lookin critter, with a blew kotton umbreller under her arm — "do you know who we air Sir?"

"My impreshun is," sed I, "from a kersery view, that you air females."

"We air, Sur," said the feroshus woman — "we belong to a Society whitch beleeves wimin has rites — which beleeves in razin her to her proper speer — whitch beleeves she is indowed with as much intelleck as man is — whitch beleeves she is trampled on and aboozed — & who will resist henso4th & forever the incroachments of proud & domineering men."

Durin her discourse, the exsentric female grabed me by the coat-kollor & was swinging her umbreller wildly over my hed.

"I hope, marm, sez I, starting back, "that your intensions is honorable? I'm a lone man hear in a strange place. Besides, Ive a wife to hum."

"Yes," cried the female, "& she's a slave! Doth she never dream of freedom — doth she never think of throwin of the yoke of tyrrinny & thinkin & votin for herself? — Doth she never think of these here things?"

"Not bein a natral born fool," sed I, by this time a little riled, "I kin safely say that she dothunt."

"O whot — whot!" screamed the female, swingin her umbreller in the air. O, what is the price that woman pays for her expeeriunce!"

"I don't know," sez I; "the price to my show is 15 cents pur individooal."

"& can't our Sosiety go in free?" asked the female.

"Not if I know it," sed I.

"Crooil, crooil man!" she cried, & bust into teers.

"Won't you let my darter in?" sed anuther of the exsentric wimin, taken me afeckshunitely by the hand. "O, please let my darter in, — shee's a sweet gushin child of natur."

"Let her gush!" roared I, as mad as I cood stick at their tarnal nonsense; "let her gush!" Where upon they all sprung back with the simultanious observashun that I was a Beest.

"My female friends," sed I, "be4 you leeve, Ive a few remarks to remark; wa them well. The female woman is one of the greatest institooshuns of which this land can boste. It's onpossible to get along without her. Had there bin no female wimin in the world, I should scarcely be here with my unparaleld show on this very occashun. She is good in sickness — good in wellness — good all the time O, woman, woman !" I cried, my feelins worked up to a hi poetick pitch, " you air a angle when you behave yourself ; but when you take off your proper appairel & (mettyforically speaken) — get into pantyloons — when you desert your firesides, & with your heds full of wimin's rites noshuns go round like roarin lyons, seekin whom you may devour somebody — in short, when you undertake to play the man, you play the devil and air an emfatic noosance. My female friends," I continnered, as they were indignantly departin, " wa well what A. Ward has sed ! "

WOULD-BE SEA DOGS.

Sum of the captings on the Upper Ohio River put on a heep of airs. To hear 'em git orf saler lingo you'd spose they'd bin on the briny Deep for a life time, when the fact is they haint tasted salt water since they was infants, when they had to take it for *worms*. Still they air good natered fellers, and when they drink they take a dose big enuff for a grown person.

ON "FORTS."

Every man has got a Fort. It's sum men's fort to do one thing, and sum other men's fort to do another, while there is numeris shiftliss critters goin round loose whose fort is not to do nothin.

Shakspeer rote good plase, but he wouldn't hav succeeded as a Washington correspondent of a New York daily paper. He lackt the rekesit fancy and imagginashun.

That's so!

Old George Washington's Fort was to not hev eny public man of the present day resemble him to eny alarmin extent. Whare bowts can George's ekal be fownd? I ask, & boldly anser no whares, or eny whare else.

Old man Townsin's Fort was to maik Sassyperiller. "Goy to the world! anuther life saived!" (Cotashun from Townsin's advertisemunt.)

ARTEMUS RESCOOD FROM THE KANAWL. [*See Page* 128.]

Cyrus Field's Fort is to lay a sub-machine tellegraf under the boundin billers of the Oshun, and then hev it Bust.

Spaldin's Fort is to maik Prepared Gloo, which mends everything. Wonder ef it will mend a sinner's wickid waze. (Impromptoo goak.)

Zoary's Fort is to be a femaile circus feller.

My Fort is the grate moral show bizniss & ritin choice famerly literatoor for the noospapers. That's what's the matter with *me.*

&c., &c., &c. So I mite go on to a indefnit extent.

Twict I've endeverd to do things which thay wasn't my Fort. The fust time was when I undertuk to lick a owdashus cuss who cut a hole in my tent & krawld threw. Sez I, "my jentle Sir go out or I shall fall onto you putty hevy." Sez he, "Wade in, Old wax figgers," whareupon I went for him, but he cawt me powerful on the hed & knockt me threw the tent into a cow pastur. He pursood the attack & flung me into a mud puddle. As I aroze & rung out my drencht garmints I koncluded fitin wasn't my Fort. Ile now rize the kurtin upon Seen 2nd: It is rarely seldum that I seek consolation in the Flowin Bole. But in a sertin town in Injianny in the Faul of 18——, my orgin grinder got sick with the fever & died. I never felt so ashamed in my life, & I thowt I'd hist in a few swallers of suthin strengthin. Konsequents was I histid in so much I dident zackly know whare bowts I was. I turnd my livin wild beests of Pray loose into the streets and spilt all my wax wurks. I then Bet I cood play hoss. So I hitched myself to a Kanawl bote, there bein two other hosses hitcht on also, one behind and anuther ahead of me. The driver hollerd for us to git up, and we did. But the hosses bein onused to sich a arrangemunt begun to kick & squeal and rair up. Konsequents was I was kickt vilently in the stummuck & back, and presuntly I fownd myself in the Kanawl with the other hosses, kickin & yellin like a tribe of Cusscaroorus savvijis. I was rescood, & as I was bein carrid to the tavern on a hemlock Bored I sed in a feeble voise, "Boys, playin hoss isn't my Fort."

MORUL—Never don't do nothin which isn't your Fort, for ef you do you'll find yourself splashin round in the Kanawl, figgeratively speakin.

PICCOLOMINI.

GENTS — I arroved in Cleveland on Saturday P. M. from Baldinsville jest in time to fix myself up and put on a clean biled rag to attend Miss Picklehomony's grate musical sorry at the Melodeon. The krowds which pored into the hall augured well for the show bisnis, & with cheerful sperrets I jined the enthoosiastic throng. I asked Mr. Strakhosh at the door if he parst the perfession, and he said not much he didn't, whereupon I bawt a preserved seat in the pit, & obsarving to Mr. Strakhosh that he needn't put on so many French airs becawz he run with a big show, and that he'd better let his weskut out a few inches or perhaps he'd bust hisself some fine day, I went in and squatted down. It was a sad thawt to think that in all that vast aujience Scacely a Sole had the honor of my acquaintance. "& this ere," sed I Bitturly, "is Fame! What sigerfy my wax figgers and livin wild beasts (which have no ekals) to these peple? What do thay care becawz a site of my Kangaroo is worth dubble the price of admission, and that my Snakes is as harmlis as the new born babe — all of which is strictly troo — ?" I should have gone on ralein at Fortin and things sum more, but jest then Signer Maccarony cum out and sung a hairey from sum opry or other. He had on his store close & looked putty slick, I must say. Nobody didn't understand nothin abowt what he sed, and so they applawdid him versiferusly. Then Signer Brignoly cum out and sung another hairey. He appeared to be in a Pensiv Mood & sung a Luv song I suppose, tho he may have been cussin the aujince all into a heep for aut I knewd. Then cum Mr. Maccarony agin & Miss Picklehomony herself. Thay sang a Doit together.

Now you know, gents, that I don't admire opry music. But I like Miss Picklehomony's stile. I like her gate. She suits me. Thare has bin grater singers and there has bin more bootiful wimin, but no more fassinatin young female ever longed for a new gown or side to place her hed agin a vest pattern than Maria Picklehomony. Fassinatin peple is her best holt. She was born to make hash of men's buzzums & other wimin mad becawz thay ain't Picklehomonies. Her face sparkles with amuzin cussedness & about 200 (two hundred) little bit of funny devils air continually dancin champion jigs in her eyes, said eyes bein brite enuff to lite a pipe by. How I shood like to have little Maria out on my farm in Baldinsville, Injianny, whare she cood run in the tall grass, wrastle with the boys, cut up strong at parin bees, make up faces behind the minister's back, tie auction bills to the skoolmaster's coat-tales, set all the fellers crazy after her, & holler & kick up, & go it just as much as she wanted to! But I diegress. Every time she cum canterin out I grew more and more delighted with her. When she bowed her hed I bowed mine. When she powtid her lips I powtid mine. When she larfed I larfed. When she jerked her hed back and took a larfin survey of the aujience, sendin a broadside of sassy smiles in among em, I tried to unjint myself & kollapse. When, in tellin how she drempt she lived in Marble Halls, she sed it tickled her more than all the rest to dream she loved her feller still the same, I made a effort to swaller myself; but when, in the next song, she looked strate at me & called me her Dear, I wildly told the man next to me he mite hav my close, as I shood never want 'em again no more in this world. [The Plain Dealer containin this communicashun is not to be sent to my famerly in Baldinsville under no circumstances whatsomever.]

In conclushun, Maria, I want you to do well. I know you air a nice gal at hart & you must get a good husband. He must be a man of branes and gumpshun & a good provider — a man who will luv you strong and long — a man who will luv you jest as much in your old age, when your voice is cracked like an old tea kittle & you can't get 1 of your notes discounted at 50 per sent a month, as he will now, when you are young & charmin & full of music, sunshine & fun. Don't marry a snob, Maria.

You ain't a Angel, Maria, & I am glad of it When I see angels in pettycoats I'm always sorry thay hain't got wings so they can kin quietly fly off where thay will be appreshiated. You air a woman, & a mity good one too. As for Maccarony, Brignoly, Mullenholler and them other fellers, they can take care of theirselves. Old Mac. kin make a comfortable livin choppin cord wood if his voice ever givs out, and Amodio looks as tho he mite succeed in conductin sum quiet toll gate, whare the vittles would be plenty & the labor lite.

I am preparin for the Summer Campane. I shall stay in Cleveland a few days and probly you will hear from me again ear I leave to once more becum a tosser on life's tempestuous billers, meanin the Show Bisnis.

Very Respectively Yours,

ARTEMUS WARD.

LITTLE PATTI.

The moosic which Ime most use to is the inspirin stranes of the hand orgin. I hire a artistic Italyun to grind fur me, payin him his vittles & close, & I spose it was them stranes which fust put a moosical taste into me. Like all furriners he had seen better dase, havin formerly been a Kount. But he aint of much akount now, except to turn the orgin and drink Beer, of which bevrige he can hold a churnful, *easy*.

Miss Patty is small for her size, but as the man sed abowt his wife, O Lord! She is well bilt & her complexion is what might be called a Broonetty. Her ize is a dark bay, the lashes bein long & silky. When she smiles the awjince feels like axing her to doo it sum moor, & to continner doin it 2 a indefnit extent. Her waste is one of the most bootiful wastisis ever seen. When Mister Strackhorse led her out I thawt sum pretty skool gal, who had jest graduatid frum pantalets & wire hoops, was a cumin out to read her fust composishun in public. She cum so bashful like, with her hed bowd down, & made sich a effort to arrange her lips so thayd look pretty, that I wanted to swaller her. She reminded me of Susan Skinner, who'd never kiss the boys at parin bees till the candles was blow'd out. Miss Patty sung suthin or ruther in a furrin tung. I don't know what the sentimunts was. Fur awt I know she may hav bin denouncin my wax figgers & sagashus wild beests of Pray, & I don't much keer ef she did. When she opened her mowth a army of martingales, bobolinks, kanarys, swallers, mockin birds, etsettery, bust 4th & flew all over the Haul.

Go it, little 1, sez I to myself, in a hily exsited frame of mind, & ef that kount or royal duke which you'll be pretty apt to marry 1 of these dase don't do the fair thing by ye, yu kin always hav a home on A. Ward's farm, near Baldinsville, Injianny.

When she sung Cumin threw the Rye, & spoke of that Swayne she deerly luvd herself individooully, I didn't wish I was that air Swayne. No I gess not. Oh certainly not. [This is Ironical. I don't meen this. It's a way I hav of goakin.] Now that Maria Picklehominy has got married [which I hopes she likes it] & left the perfeshun, Adeliny Patty is the championess of the opery ring. She karries the Belt. Thar's no draw fite about it. Other primy donnys may as well throw up the spunge first as last. My eyes don't deceive my earsite in this matter.

But Miss Patty orter sing in the Inglish tung. As she kin do so as well as she kin in Italyun why under the Son dont she do it? What cents is thare in singin wurds nobody dont understan when wurds we do understan is jest as handy? Why peple will versifferusly applawd furrin langwidge is a mistery. It reminds me of a man I onct knew. He sed he knockt the bottum out of his pork Barril, & the pork fell out, but the Brine dident moove a inch. It stade in the Barril. He sed this was a Mistery, but it wasn't misterior than is this thing I'm speekin of.

As fur Brignoly, Ferri and Junky, thay air dowtless grate, but I think sich able boddied men wood look better tillin the sile than dressin theirselves up in black close & white kid gluvs & shoutin in a furrin tung. Mister Junky is a noble lookin old man & orter lead armies on to Battel instid of shoutin in a furrin tung.

Adoo. In the langwidge of Lewis Napoleon when receivin kumpany at his pallis on the Bullyvards, "I saloot yu."

"Oh that I should live to see myself a ded body!" screamed the unfortnet man. [*See Page* 145.]

MOSES, THE SASSY; OR, THE DISGUISED DUKE.

CHAPTER I. — ELIZY.

My story opens in the classic presinks of Bostin. In the parler of a bloated aristocratic mansion on Bacon street sits a luvly young lady, whose hair is cuverd ore with the frosts of between 17 Summers. She has just sot down to the piany, and is warblin the popler ballad called "Smells of the Notion," in which she tells how with pensiv thought, she wandered by a C beat shore. The son is settin in its horizon, and its gorjus light pores in a golden meller flud through the winders, and makes the young lady twict as beautiful nor what she was before, which is onnecessary. She is magnificently dressed up in a Berage basque, with poplin trimmins, More Antique, Ball Morals and 3 ply carpeting. Also, considerable gauze. Her dress contains 16 flounders and her shoes is red morocker, with gold spangles onto them. Presently she jumps up with a wild snort, and pressin her hands to her brow, she exclaims: "Methinks I see a voice!"

A noble youth of 27 summers enters. He is attired in a red shirt and black trowsis, which last air turned up over his boots; his hat, which it is a plug, being cockt onto one side of his classical hed. In sooth, he was a heroic lookin person, with a fine shape. Grease, in its barmiest days near projuced a more hefty cavileer. Gazin upon him admirinly for a spell, Elizy (for that was her name) organized herself into a tabloo, and stated as follers.

"Ha! do me eyes deceive me earsight? Is it some dreams? No, I reckon not! That frame! them store close! those nose! Yes, it is me own, me only Moses!"

He (Moses) folded her to his hart, with the remark that he was "a hunkey boy."

CHAPTER II.—Was Moses of Noble Birth ?

Moses was foreman of Engine Co. No. 40. Forty's fellers had just bin havin an annual re-union with Fifty's fellers, on the day I introjuce Moses to my readers, and Moses had his arms full of trofees, to wit : 4 scalps, 5 eyes, 3 fingers, 7 ears, (which he chawed off) and several half and quarter sections of noses. When the fair Elizy re-covered from her delight at meetin Moses, she said : — " How hast the battle gonest? Tell me ! "

" We chawed 'em up — that's what we did ! " said the bold Moses.

" I thank the gods ! " sed the fair Elizy. " Thou did'st excellent well. And, Moses," she continnered, layin her hed confidinly agin his weskit, " dost know I sumtimes think thou istest of noble birth ? "

" No ! " said he, wildly ketchin hold of hisself. " Yóu don't say so ! "

" Indeed do I ! Your dead grandfather's sperrit comest to me the tother night."

" Oh no, I guess it's a mistake," sed Moses.

"I'll bet two dollars and a quarter he did!" replied Elizy. "He said, 'Moses is a Disguised Juke!'"

"You mean Duke," said Moses.

"Dost not the actors all call it Juke!" said she.

That settled the matter.

"I hav thought of this thing afore," said Moses, abstractedly. "If it is so, then thus it must be! 2 B or not 2 B! Which? Sow, sow! But enuff. O life! life! — *you're too many for me!*" He tore out some of his pretty yeller hair, stampt on the floor sevril times, and was gone.

CHAPTER III.—The Pirut Foiled.

Sixteen long and weary years has elapst since the seens narrated in the last chapter took place. A noble ship, the Sary Jane, is a sailin from France to Ameriky via the Wabash Canal. A pirut ship is in hot pursoot of the Sary. The pirut capting isn't a man of much principle and intends to kill all the people on bored the Sary and confiscate the wallerbles. The capting of the S. J. is on the pint of givin in, when a fine lookin feller in russet boots and a buffalo overcoat rushes forored and obsarves:

"Old man! go down stairs! Retire to the starbud bulk-hed! I'll take charge of this Bote!"

"Owdashus cuss!" yelled the capting, "away with thee or I shall do mur-rer-der-r-r!"

"Skurcely," obsarved the stranger, and he drew a diamond-hilted fish-knife and cut orf the capting's hed. He expired shortly, his last words bein, "we are governed too much."

"People!" sed the stranger, "I'm the Juke d'Moses!"

"Old hoss!" sed a passenger, "methinks thou art blowin!" whareupon the Juke cut orf his hed also.

"Oh that I should live to see myself a ded body!" screamed the unfortnit man. "But don't print any verses about my deth in the newspapers, for if you do I'll haunt ye!"

"People!" sed the Juke, "I alone can save you from yon bloody pirut! Ho! a peck of oats!" The oats was brought, and the Juke, boldly mountin the jibpoop, throwed them onto the towpath. The pirut rapidly approached, chucklin with fiendish delight at the idee of increasin his ill-gotten gains. But the leadin hoss of the pirut ship stopt suddent on comin to the oats, and commenst for to devour them. In vain the piruts swore and throwd stones and bottles at the hoss — he wouldn't budge a inch. Meanwhile the Sary Jane, her hosses on the full jump, was fast leavin the pirut ship !

"Onct agin do I escape deth !" sed the Juke between his clencht teeth, still on the jibpoop.

CHAPTER IV. — The Wanderer's Return.

The Juke was Moses the Sasy ! Yes, it was !

He had bin to France and now he was home agin in Bostin, which gave birth to a Bunker Hill ! ! He had some trouble in gitting hisself acknowledged as Juke in France, as the Orleans Dienasty and Borebones were fernest him, but he finally conkered. Elizy knowd him right off, as one of his ears and a part of his nose had bin chawed off in his fights with opposition firemen durin boyhood's sunny hours. They lived to a green old age, beloved by all, both grate and small. Their children, of which they have numerous, often go up onto the Common and see the Fountain squirt.

This is my 1st attempt at writin a Tail & it is far from bein perfeck, but if I have indoosed folks to see that in 9 cases out of 10 they can either make Life as barren as the Dessert of Sarah, or as joy-yus as a flower garding, my objeck will have bin accomplished, and more too.

THE PRINCE OF WALES.

To my friends of the Editorial Corpse:

I rite these lines on British sile. I've bin follerin Mrs. Victory's hopeful sun Albert Edward threw Kanady with my onparaleled Show, and tho I haint made much in a pecoonery pint of vew, I've lernt sumthin new, over hear on British Sile, whare they bleeve in Saint Gorge and the Dragoon. Previs to cumin over hear I tawt my organist how to grind Rule Brittanny and other airs which is poplar on British Sile. I likewise fixt a wax figger up to represent Sir Edmun Hed the Govner Ginral. The statoot I fixt up is the most versytile wax statoot I ever saw. I've showd it as Wm. Penn, Napoleon Bonypart, Juke of Wellington, the Beneker Boy, Mrs. Cunningham & varis other notid persons, & also for a sertin pirut named Hix. I've bin so long amung wax statoots that I can fix 'em up to soot the tastes of folks, & with sum paints I hav I kin giv their facis a beneverlent or fiendish look as the kase requires. I giv Sir Edmun Hed a beneverlent look, & when sum folks who thawt they was smart sed it didn't look like Sir Edmun Hed anymore than it did anybody else, I sed, "That's the pint. That's the beauty of the Statoot. It looks like Sir Edmun Hed or any other man. You may kall it what you pleese. Ef it don't look like anybody that ever lived, then it's sertinly a remarkable Statoot & well worth seein. *I* kall it Sir Edmun Hed. *You* may kall it what you darn pleese!" [I had 'em thare.]

At larst I've had a interview with the Prince, tho it putty nigh cost me my vallerble life. I cawt a glimps of him as he sot on the Pizarro of the hotel in Sarnia, & elbowd myself threw a crowd of wimin, children, sojers & Injins that was hangin round the tavern. I was drawin near to the Prince when a red faced man in Millingtery close grabd holt of me and axed me whare I was goin all so bold?

"To see Albert Edard the Prince of Wales," sez I; "who are you?"

He sed he was Kurnel of the Seventy Fust Regiment, Her Magisty's troops. I told him I hoped the Seventy Onesters was in good helth, and was passin by when he ceased hold of me agin, and sed in a tone of indigent cirprise:

"What? Impossible! It kannot be! Blarst my hize, sir, did I understan you to say that you was actooally goin into the presents of his Royal Iniss?"

"That's what's the matter with me," I replide.

"But blarst my hize, sir, its onprecedented. It's orful, sir. Nothin' like it hain't happened sins the Gun Power Plot of Guy Forks. Owdashus man, who air yu?"

"Sir," sez I, drawin myself up & puttin on a defiant air, "I'm a Amerycan sitterzen. My name is Ward. I'm a husband & the father of twins, which I'm happy to state thay look like me. By perfeshun I'm a exhibiter of wax works & sich."

"Good God!" yelled the Kurnal, "the idee of

a exhibiter of wax figgers goin into the presents of Royalty! The British Lion may well roar--with raje at the thawt!"

Sez I, "Speakin of the British Lion, Kurnal, I'd like to make a bargin with you fur that beast fur a few weeks to add to my Show." I didn't meen nothin by this. I was only gettin orf a goak, but you orter hev seen the Old Kurnal jump up & howl. He actooally fomed at the mowth.

"This can't be real," he showtid. "No, no. It's a horrid dream. Sir, you air not a human bein — you hav no existents — yure a Myth!"

"Wall," sez I, "old hoss, yule find me a ruther onkomfortable Myth ef you punch my inards in that way agin." I began to git a little riled, fur when he called me a Myth he puncht me putty hard. The Kurnal now commenst showtin fur the Seventy Onesters. I at fust thawt I'd stay & becum a Marter to British Outraje, as sich a course mite git my name up & be a good advertisement fur my Show, but it occurred to me that ef enny of the Seventy Onesters shood happen to insert a barronet into my stummick it mite be onplesunt, & I was on the pint of runnin orf when the Prince hisself kum up & axed me what the matter was. Sez I, "Albert Edard is that you?" & he smilt & sed it was. Sez I, "Albert Edard, hears my keerd. I cum to pay my respecks to the futer King of Ingland. The Kurnal of the Seventy Onesters hear is ruther smawl pertaters, but of course you ain't to blame fur that. He puts on as many airs as tho he was the Bully Boy with the glass eye."

"Never mind," sez Albert Edard, "I'm glad to see you, Mister Ward, at all events," & he tuk my hand so plesunt like & larfed so sweet that I fell in love with him to onct. He handid me a segar & we sot down on the Pizarro & commenst smokin rite cheerful. "Wall," sez I, "Albert Edard, how's the old folks?"

"Her Majesty & the Prince are well," he sed.

"Duz the old man take his Lager beer reglar?" I inquired.

The Prince larfed & intermatid that the old man didn't let many kegs of that bevridge spile in the sellar in the coarse of a year. We sot & tawked there sum time abowt matters & things, & bimeby I axed him how he liked bein Prince as fur as h'ed got.

"To speak plain, Mister Ward," he sed, "I don't much like it. I'm sick of all this bowin & scrapin & crawlin & hurrain over a boy like me. I would rather go through the country quietly & enjoy myself in my own way, with the other boys, & not be made a Show of to be garped at by every-body. When the *peple* cheer me I feel pleesed, fur I know they meen it, but if these one-horse offishuls cood know how I see threw all their moves & un-derstan exackly what they air after, & knowd how I larft at 'em in private, thayd stop kissin my hands & fawnin over me as thay now do. But you know Mr. Ward I can't help bein a Prince, & I must do all I kin to fit myself fur the persishun I must sumtime ockepy."

"That's troo," sez I; "sickness and the docters will carry the Queen orf one of these dase, sure's yer born."

The time hevin arove fur me to take my departer I rose up & sed: "Albert Edard, I must go, but previs to doin so I will obsarve that you soot me. Yure a good feller Albert Edard, & tho I'm agin Princes as a gineral thing, I must say I like the cut of your Gib. When you git to be King try and be as good a man as yure muther has bin.! Be just & be Jenerus, espeshully to showmen, who hav allers bin aboozed sins the dase of Noah, who was the fust man to go into the Menagery bizniss, & ef the daily papers of his time air to be beleeved Noah's colleck-shun of livin wild beests beet ennything ever seen sins, tho I make bold to dowt ef his snaiks was ahead of mine. Albert Edard, adoo!" I tuk his hand which he shook warmly, & givin him a perpet-ooal free pars to my show, & also parses to take hum for the Queen & Old Albert, I put on my hat and walkt away

"Mrs. Ward," I solilerquized, as I walkt along, "Mrs. Ward, ef you could see your husband now, just as he prowdly emerjis from the presunts of the futur King of Ingland, you'd be sorry you called him a Beest jest becaws he cum home tired 1 nite and wantid to go to bed without takin orf his boots. You'd be sorry for tryin to deprive yure husband of the priceliss Boon of liberty, Betsy Jane ! "

Jest then I met a long perseshun of men with gownds onto 'em. The leader was on horseback, & ridin up to me he sed, " Air you Orange ? "

Sez I, " Which ? "

" Air you a Orangeman ? " he repeated, sternly.

" I used to peddle lemins," sed I, " but I never delt in oranges. They are apt to spile on yure hands. What particler Loonatic Asylum hev you & yure frends escaped frum, ef I may be so bold ? " Just then a suddent thawt struck me & I sed, " Oh yure the fellers who air worryin the Prince so & givin the Juke of Noocastle cold sweats at nite, by yure infernal catawalins, air you ? Wall, take the advice of a Amerykin sitterzen, take orf them gownds & don't try to get up a religious fite, which is 40 times wuss nor a prize fite, over Albert Edard, who wants to receive you all on a ekal footin, not keerin a tinker's cuss what meetin house you sleep in Sundays. Go home and mind yure bisness & not make noosenses of yourselves." With which observashuns I left 'em.

I shall leeve British sile 4thwith.

OSSAWATOMIE BROWN.

I don't pertend to be a cricket & consekently the reader will not regard this 'ere peace as a Cricket-cism. I cimply desine givin the pints & Plot of a play I saw actid out at the theater t'other nite, called Ossywattermy Brown or the Hero of Harper's Ferry. Ossywattermy had varis failins, one of which was a idee that he cood conker Virginny with a few duzzen loonatics which he had pickt up sumwhares, mercy only nose wheu. He didn't cum it, as the sekel showed. This play was jerkt by a admirer of Old Ossywattermy.

First akt opens at North Elby, Old Brown's humsted. Thare's a weddin at the house. Amely, Old Brown's darter, marrys sumbody, and they all whirl in the Messy darnce. Then Ossywattermy and his 3 suns leave fur Kansis. Old Mrs. Ossywattermy tells 'em thay air goin on a long jurny & Blesses 'em to slow fiddlin. Thay go to Kansis. What upon arth thay go to Kansis fur when thay was so nice & comfortable down there to North Elby, is more'n I know. The suns air next seen in Kansis at a tarvern. Mister Blane, a sinister lookin man with his Belt full of knives & hoss pistils, axes one of the Browns to take a drink. Brown refuzis, which is the fust instance on record whar a Brown deklined sich a invite. Mister Blane, who is a dark bearded feroshus lookin person, then axis him whether he's fur or fernenst Slavery. Yung Brown sez he's agin it, whareupon Mister Blane, who is the most sinisterest lookin man I ever saw, sez Har, har, har! (that bein his stile of larfin wildly) & ups & sticks a knife into yung Brown. Anuther Brown rushes up & sez, "you has killed me Ber-ruther!" Moosic by the Band & Seen changes. The stuck yung Brown enters supported by his two brothers. Bimeby he falls down, sez he sees his Mother, & dies. Moosic by the Band. I lookt but couldn't see any mother. Next Seen reveels Old

Brown's cabin. He's readin a book. He sez freedum must extend its Area & rubs his hands like he was pleesed abowt it. His suns come in. One of 'em goes out & cums in ded, havin bin shot while out by a Border Ruffin. The ded yung Brown sez he sees his mother and tumbles down. The Border Ruffins then surround the cabin & set it a fire. The Browns giv theirselves up for gone coons, when the hired gal diskivers a trap door to the cabin & thay go down threw it & cum up threw the bulkhed. Their merraklis 'scape reminds me of the 'scape of De Jones the Coarsehair of the Gulf — a tail with a yaller kiver, that I onct red. For sixteen years he was confined in a loathsum dunjin, not tastin of food durin all that time. When a lucky thawt struck him! He opend the winder and got out. To resoom — Old Brown rushes down to the footlites, gits down on his nees & swares he'll hav revenge. The battle of Ossawattermy takes place. Old Brown kills Mister Blane, the sinister individooal aforesed. Mister Blane makes a able & elerquent speech, sez he don't see his mother *much*, and dies like a son of a gentleman, rapt up in the Star Spangled Banner. Moosic by the Band. Four or five other Border ruffins air killed but thay don't say nothin abowt seein their mothers. From Kansis to Harper's Ferry. Picter of a Arsenal is represented. Sojers cum & fire at it. Old Brown cums out & permits hisself to be shot. He is tride by two soops in milingtery close, and sentenced to be hung on the gallus. Tabloo — Old Brown on a platform, pintin upards, the staige lited up with red fire. Goddiss of Liberty also on platform, pintin upards. A dutchman in the orkestry warbles on a base drum. Curtin falls. Moosic by the Band.

"TWINS, MARM," SEZ I, "TWINS!" [*See Page* 165.

JOY IN THE HOUSE OF WARD.

Dear Sirs : —

I take my pen in hand to inform you that I am in a state of grate bliss, and trust these lines will find you injoyin the same blessins. I'm reguvinated. I've found the immortal waters of yooth, so to speak, and am as limber and frisky as a two-year old steer, and in the futer them boys which sez to me "go up, old Bawld hed," will do so at the peril of their hazard, individooally. I'm very happy. My house is full of joy, and I have to git up nights and larf! Sumtimes I ax myself "is it not a dream?" & suthin withinto me sez "it air;" but when I look at them sweet little critters and hear 'em squawk, I know it is a reality — 2 realitys, I may say — and I feel gay.

I returnd from the Summer Campane with my unparaleld show of wax works and livin wild Beests of Pray in the early part of this munth. The peple of Baldinsville met me cordully and I immejitly commenst restin myself with my famerly. The other nite while I was down to the tavurn tostin my shins agin the bar room fire & amuzin the krowd with sum of my adventurs, who shood cum in bare heded & terrible excited but Bill Stokes, who sez, sez he, "Old Ward, there's grate doins up to your house."

Sez I, "William, how so?"

Sez he, "Bust my gizzud, but its grate doins," & then he larfed as if hee'd kill hisself.

Sez I, risin and puttin on a austeer look, "William, I woodunt be a fool if I had common cents."

But he kept on larfin till he was black in the face, when he fell over on to the bunk where the hostler sleeps, and in a still small voice sed, "Twins!" I ashure you gents that the grass didn't grow under my feet on my way home, & I was follered by a enthoosiastic throng of my feller sitterzens, who hurrard for Old Ward at the top of their voises. I found the house chock full of peple.

Thare was Mis Square Baxter and her three grown up darters, lawyer Perkinses wife, Taberthy Ripley young Eben Parsuns, Deakun Simmuns folks, the Skoolmaster, Doctor Jordin, etsettery, etsettery. Mis Ward was in the west room, which jines the kitchin. Mis Square Baxter was mixin suthin in a dipper before the kitchin fire, & a small army of female wimin were rushin wildly round the house with bottles of camfire, peaces of flannil, &c. I never seed sich a hubbub in my natral born dase. I cood not stay in the west room only a minit, so strung up was my feelins, so I rusht out and ceased my dubbel barrild gun.

" What upon airth ales the man ? " sez Taberthy Ripley. " Sakes alive, what air you doin ? " & she grabd me by the coat tales. " What's the matter with you ? " she continnerd.

" Twins, marm," sez I, " twins ! "

" I know it," sez she, coverin her pretty face with her apun.

" Wall," sez I, " that's what's the matter with me ! "

"Wall put down that air-gun, you pesky old fool," sed she.

"No, marm," sez I, "this is a Nashunal day. The glory of this here day isn't confined to Baldinsville by a darn site. On yonder woodshed," sed I, drawin myself up to my full hite and speakin in a show actin voice, "will I fire a Nashunal saloot!" sayin whitch I tared myself from her grasp and rusht to the top of the shed whare I blazed away until Square Baxter's hired man and my son Artemus Juneyer cum and took me down by mane force.

On returnin to the Kitchin I found quite a lot of people seated be4 the fire, a talkin the event over. They made room for me & I sot down. "Quite a eppisode," sed Docter Jordin, litin his pipe with a red hot coal.

"Yes," sed I, "2 eppisodes, waying abowt 18 pounds jintly."

"A perfeck coop de tat," sed the skoolmaster.

"E pluribus unum, in proprietor persony," sed I, thinking I'd let him know I understood furrin langwidges as well as he did, if I wasn't a skoolmaster.

"It is indeed a momentious event," sed young Eben Parsuns, who has been 2 quarters to the Akademy.

"I never heard twins called by that name afore," sed I, "but I spose it's all rite."

"We shall soon have Wards enuff," sed the editer of the Baldinsville *Bugle of Liberty*, who was lookin over a bundle of exchange papers in the corner, "to apply to the legislater for a City Charter?"

"Good for you, old man!" sed I, "giv that air a conspickius place in the next *Bugle.*"

"How redicklus," sed pretty Susan Fletcher, coverin her face with her knittin work & larfin like all possest.

"Wall, for my part," sed Jane Maria Peasley who is the crossest old made in the world, "I think you all act like a pack of fools."

Sez I, "Mis. Peasly, air you a parent?"

Sez she, "No, I aint."

Sez I, 'Mis. Peasly, you never will be."

She left.

We sot there talkin & larfin until "the switchin hour of nite, when grave yards yawn & Josts troop 4th," as old Bill Shakespire aptlee obsarves in his dramy of John Sheppard, esq., or the Moral House Breaker, when we broke up & disbursed.

Muther & children is a doin well; & as Resolushuns is the order of the day I will feel obleeged if you'll insurt the follerin —

Whereas, two Eppisodes has happined up to the undersined's house, which is Twins; & Whereas I like this stile, sade twins bein of the male perswashun & both boys; there4 Be it

Resolved, that to them nabers who did the fare thing by sade Eppisodes my hart felt thanks is doo.

Resolved, that I do most hartily thank Engine Ko. No. 17 who, under the impreshun from the fuss at my house on that auspishus nite that thare was a konflagration goin on, kum galyiantly to the spot, but kindly refraned frum squirtin.

Resolved, that frum the Bottum of my Sole do I

thank the Baldinsville brass band fur givin up the idea of Sarahnadin me, both on that great nite & sinse.

Resolved, that my thanks is doo several members of the Baldinsville meetin house who fur 3 whole dase hain't kalled me a sinful skoffer or intreeted me to mend my wicked wase and jine sade meetin house to onct.

Resolved, that my Boozum teams with meny kind emoshuns towards the follerin individoouls, to whit namelee — Mis. Square Baxter, who Jenerusly refoozed to take a sent for a bottle of camfire; lawyer Perkinses wife who rit sum versis on the Eppisodes; the Editer of the Baldinsville *Bugle of Liberty*, who nobly assisted me in wollupin my Kangeroo, which sagashus little cuss seriusly disturbed the Eppisodes by his outrajus screetchins & kickins up; Mis. Hirum Doolittle, who kindly furnisht sum cold vittles at a tryin time, when it wasunt konvenient to cook vittles at my house; & the Peasleys, Parsunses & Watsunses fur there meny ax of kindness

Trooly yures, ARTEMUS WARD.

CRUISE OF THE POLLY ANN.

In overhaulin one of my old trunks the tother day, I found the follerin' jernal of a vyge on the starnch canawl bote, Polly Ann, which happened to the subscriber when I was a young man (in the Brite Lexington of yooth, when thar aint no sich word as fale) on the Wabash Canawl:

(Monday 2 P. M.) Got under wa. Hosses not remarkable frisky at fust. Had to bild fires under 'em before they'd start. Started at larst very suddent, causin the bote for to lurch vilently and knockin me orf from my pins. (Sailor frase.) Sevral passenjers on bored. Parst threw deliteful country. Honist farmers was to work sowin korn, & other projuce in the fields. Surblime scenery. Large red-heded gal reclinin on the banks of the Canawl, bathin her feet.

Turned in at 15 minits parst eleving.

Toosdy — Riz at 5 and went up on the poop deck. Took a grown person's dose of licker with a member of the Injianny legislater, which he urbanely insisted on allowin me to pay for. Bote tearin threu the briny waters at the rate of 2 Nots a hour, when the boy on the leadin hoss shoutid,

"Sale hoe!"

"Whar away?" hollered the capting, clearin his glass (a empty black bottle, with the bottom knockt out) and bringing it to his Eagle eye.

"Bout four rods to the starbud," screamed the boy.

"Jes so," screeched the capting. "What wessel's that air?"

"Kickin Warier of Terry Hawt, and be darned to you!"

"I, I Sir!" hollered our capting. "Reef your arft hoss, splice your main jib-boom, and hail your chambermaid! What's up in Terry Hawt?"

"You know Bill Spikes?" sed the capting of the Warier.

"Wall, I reckin He kan eat more fride pork

nor any man of his heft on the Wabash. He's a ornament to his sex!"

"Wall," continued the capting of the Kickin Marier. "Wilyim got a little owly the tother day, and got to prancin around town on that old white mare of his'r, and bein in a playful mood, he rid up in front of the Court 'us whar old Judge Perkins was a holdin Court, and let drive his rifle at him. The bullet didn't hit the Judge at all; it only jes whizzed parst his left ear, lodgin in the wall behind him; but what d'ye spose the old despot did? Why, he actooally fined Bill ten dollars for contempt of Court! What do you think of that?" axed the capting of the Marier, as he parst a long black bottle over to our capting.

"The country is indeed in danger!" sed our capting, raisin the bottle to his lips. The wessels parted. No other incidents that day. Retired to my chased couch at 5 minits parst 10.

(Wensdy.) Riz arly. Wind blowin N. W. E. Hevy sea on and ship rollin wildly in consekents of pepper-corns havin bin fastened to the forrerd hoss's tale. "Heave two!" roared the capting to the man at the rudder, as the Polly giv a friteful toss. I was sick, an sorry I'd cum. "Heave two!" repeated the capting. I went below. "Heave two!" I hearn him holler agin, and stickin my hed out of the cabin winder, *I hev.*

The hosses became dosile eventually, and I felt better. The sun bust out in all his splender, disregardless of expense, and lovely Natur put in her best licks. We parst the beautiful village of Limy, which lookt sweet indeed, with its neat white cottages, Institoots of learnin and other evijences of civillizashun, incloodin a party of bald heded cullered men who was playing 3 card monty on the stoop of the Red Eagle tavern. All, all was food for my 2 poetic sole. I went below to breakfast, but vittles had lost their charms. "Take sum of this," sed the Capting, shovin a bottle tords my plate. "It's whisky. A few quarts allers sets me right when my stummick gits out of order. It's a excellent tonic!" I declined the seductive flooid.

(Thursdy.) Didn't rest well last night on account of a uprore made by the capting, who stopt the Bote to go ashore and smash in the windows of a grosery. He was brought back in about a hour, with his hed dun up in a red hankercher, his eyes bein swelled up orful, and his nose very much out of jint. He was bro't aboard on a shutter by his crue, and deposited on the cabin floor, the passenjers all risin up in their births, pushin the red curtains aside & lookin out to see what the matter was. "Why do you allow your pashuns to run away with you in this onseemly stile, my misgided frend?" sed a sollum lookin man in a red flannel nite-cap. "Why do you sink yourself to the Beasts of the field?"

"Wall, the fack is," sed the capting, risin hisself on the shutter, "I've bin a little prejoodiced agin that grosery for some time. But I made it lively for the boys, Deacon! Bet yer life!" He larfed a short, wild larf, and called for his jug. Sippin a few pints, he smiled gently upon the passengers, sed "Bless you! bless you!" and fell into a sweet sleep.

Eventually we reached our jerny's end. This was in the days of Old Long Sign, be4 the iron hoss was foaled. This was be4 steembotes was goin round bustin their bilers & sendin peple higher nor a kite. Them was happy days when peple was intelligent & wax figger's & livin wild beests wasn't scoffed at.

"O dase of me boyhood
I'm dreamin on ye now!"

(Poeckry.) A. W.

INTERVIEW WITH PRESIDENT LINCOLN.

I hav no politics. Nary a one. I'm not in the bisiness. If I was I spose I should holler versiff-rusly in the streets at nite and go home to Betsy Jane smellen of coal ile and gin, in the mornin. I should go to the Poles arly. I should stay there all day. I should see to it that my nabers was thar. I should git carriges to take the kripples, the infirm and the indignant thar. I should be on guard agin frauds and sich. I should be on the look out for the infamus lise of the enemy, got up jest be4 elec-shun for perlitical effeck. When all was over and my candydate was elected, I should move heving & arth — so to speak — until I got orfice, which if I didn't git a orfice I should turn round and abooze the Administration with all my mite and maine. But

AN INTERVIEW WITH PRESIDENT LINCOLN. [*See Page* 186.]

I'm not in the bisniss. I'm in a far more respectful bisniss nor what pollertics is. I wouldn't giv two cents to be a Congresser. The wuss insult I ever received was when sertin citizens of Baldinsville axed me to run fur the Legislater. Sez I, My frends, dostest think I'd stoop to that there?" They turned as white as a sheet. I spoke in my most orfullest tones, & they knowd I wasn't to be trifled with. They slunked out of site to onct.

There4, havin no politics, I made bold to visit Old Abe at his humstid in Springfield. I found the old feller in his parler, surrounded by a perfeck swarm of orfice seekers. Knowin he had been capting of a flat boat on the roarin Mississippy I thought I'd address him in sailor lingo, so sez I "Old Abe, ahoy! Let out yer main-suls, reef hum the fore-castle & throw yer jib-poop over-board! Shiver my timbers, my harty!" [N. B. This is ginu-ine mariner langwidge. I know, becawz I've seen sailor plays acted out by them New York theater fellers.] Old Abe lookt up quite cross & sez, "Send in yer petition by & by. I can't possibly look at it now. Indeed, I can't. It's onpossible, sir!"

"Mr. Linkin, who do you spect I air?" sed I.

"A orfice-seeker, to be sure?" sed he.

"Wall, sir," sed I, "you s never more mistaken in your life. You hain't gut a orfiss I'd take under no circumstances. I'm A. Ward. Wax figgers is my perfeshun. I'm the father of Twins, and they look like me — *both of them.* I cum to pay a frendly visit to the President eleck of the United States. If so be you wants to see me say so — if not, say so, & I'm orf like a jug handle."

"Mr. Ward, sit down. I am glad to see you, Sir."

"Repose in Abraham's Buzzum!" sed one of the orfice seekers, his idee bein to git orf a goak at my expense.

"Wall," sez I, "ef all you fellers repose in that there Buzzum thare'll be mity poor nussin for sum of you!" whereupon Old Abe buttoned his weskit clear up and blusht like a maidin of sweet 16. Jest at this pint of the conversation another swarm of orfice-seekers arrove & cum pilin into the parler. Sum wanted post orfices, sum wanted collectorships sum wantid furrin missions, and all wanted sumthin. I thought Old Abe would go crazy. He hadn't more than had time to shake hands with 'em, before another tremenjis crowd cum porein onto his premises. His house and dooryard was now perfeckly overflowed with orfice seekers, all clameruss for a immejit interview with Old Abe. One man from Ohio, who had about seven inches of corn whisky into him, mistook me for Old Abe and addrest me as "The Pra-hayrie Flower of the West!" Thinks I *you* want a offiss putty bad. Another man with a gold heded cane and a red nose told Old Abe he was "a seckind Washington & the Pride of the Boundliss West."

Sez I, "Square, you wouldn't take a small post-offis if you could git it, would you?"

Sez he, "a patrit is abuv them things, sir!"

"There's a putty big crop of patrits this season, aint there Squire?" sez I, when *another* crowd of offiss seekers pored in. The house, door-yard, barn

& woodshed was now all full, and when *another* crowd cum I told 'em not to go away for want of room as the hog-pen was still empty. One patrit from a small town in Michygan went up on top the house, got into the chimney and slid down intc the parler where Old Abe was endeverin to keep the hungry pack of orfice-seekers from chawin him up alive without benefit of clergy. The minit he reached the fire-place he jumpt up, brusht the soot out of his eyes, and yelled: "Don't make eny pintment at the Spunkville postoffiss till you've read my papers. All the respectful men in our town is signers to that there dockyment!"

"Good God!" cride Old Abe, "they cum upon me from the skize — down the chimneys, and from the bowels of the yearth!" He hadn't more'n got them words out of his delikit mouth before two fat offiss-seekers from Wisconsin, in endeverin to crawl atween his legs for the purpuss of applyin for the tollgateship at Milwawky, upsot the President eleck & he would hev gone sprawlin into the fire-place if I hadn't caught him in these arms. But I hadn't morn'n stood him up strate before another man cum crashin down the chimney, his head strikin me vilently agin the inards and prostratin my voluptoous form onto the floor. "Mr. Linkin," shoutid the infatooated being, "my papers is signed by every clergyman in our town, and likewise the skoolmaster!"

Sez I, "you egrejis ass," gittin up & brushin the dust from my eyes, "I'll sign your papers with this bunch of bones, if you don't be a little more keerful how you make my bread basket a depot in the futer. How do you like that air perfumery?" sez I, shuving my fist under his nose. "Them's the kind of papers I'll giv you! Them's the paper's *you* want!"

"But I workt hard for the ticket; I toiled night and day! The patrit should be rewarded!"

"Virtoo," sed I, holdin' the infatooated man by the coat-collar, "virtoo, sir, is its own reward. Look at me!" He did look at me, and qualed be4 my gase. "The fact is," I continued, lookin' round on the hungry crowd, "there is scacely a offiss for every ile lamp carrid round durin' this campane. I wish thare was. I wish thare was furrin missions to be filled on varis lonely Islands where eppydemics rage incessantly, and if I was in Old Abe's place I'd send every mother's son of you to them. What air you here for?" I continnered, warmin up considerable, "can't you giv Abe a minit's peace? Don't you see he's worrid most to death! Go home, you miserable men, go home & till the sile! Go to peddlin tinware — go to choppin wood — go to bilin' sope — stuff sassengers — black boots — git a clerkship on sum respectable manure cart — go round as original Swiss Bell Ringers — becum 'origenal and only' Campbell Minstrels — go to lecturin at 50 dollars a nite — imbark in the peanut bizniss — *write for the Ledger* — saw off your legs and go round givin concerts, with techin appeals to a charitable public, printed on your handbills — anything for a honest living, but don't come round here drivin Old Abe crazy by your outrajis cuttings up! Go home. Stand not upon the order of your goin,' but go to onct! If in five minits from this time," sez I pullin' out my new sixteen dollar huntin cased watch, and brandishin' it before their eyes, "Ef in five minits from this time a single sole of you remains on these here premises, I'll go out to my cage near by, and let my Boy Constructor loose! & ef he gits amung you, you'll think old Solferino has cum again and no mistake!" You ought to hev seen them scamper, Mr. Fair. They run orf as tho Satun his self was arter them with a red hot ten pronged pitchfork. In five minits the premises was clear.

"How kin I ever repay you, Mr. Ward, for your kindness?" sed Old Abe, advancin and shakin me warmly by the hand. "How kin I ever repay you, sir?"

"By givin the whole country a good, sound administration. By poerin' ile upon the troubled waturs, North and South. By pursooin' a patriotic, firm, and just course, and then if any State wants to secede, let 'em Sesesh!"

"How 'bout my Cabinit, Mister, Ward?" sed Abe.

"Fill it up with Showmen sir! Showmen is

devoid of politics. They hain't got any principles! They know how to cater for the public. They know what the public wants, North & South. Showmen, sir, is honest men. Ef you doubt their literary ability, look at their posters, and see small bills! Ef you want a Cabinit as is a Cabinit fill it up with showmen, but don't call on me. The moral wax figger perfeshun musn't be permitted to go down while there's a drop of blood in these vains! A. Linkin, I wish you well! Ef Powers or Walcutt wus to pick out a model for a beautiful man, I scarcely think they'd sculp you; but ef you do the fair thing by your country you'll make as putty a angel as any of us! A. Linkin, use the talents which Nature has put into you judishusly and firmly, and all will be well! A. Linkin, adoo!"

He shook me cordyully by the hand — we exchanged picters, so we could gaze upon each others' liniments when far away from one another — he at the hellum of the ship of State, and I at the hellum of the show bizniss — admittance only 15 cents.

"I was ceased and tied to a stump." [*See Page* 193.]

THE SHOW IS CONFISCATED.

You hav perhaps wondered wharebouts I was foi these many dase gone and past. Perchans you sposed I'd gone to the Tomb of the Cappylets, tho I don't know what those is. It's a popler noospaper frase.

Listen to my tail, and be silent that ye may here. I've been among the Seseshers, a earnin my daily peck by my legitimit perfeshun, and havn't had no time to weeld my facile quill for "the Grate Komick paper," if you'll alow me to kote from your troothful advertisement.

My success was skaly, and I likewise had a narrer scape of my life. If what I've bin threw is "Suthern hosspitality," 'bout which we've hearn so much, then I feel bound to obsarve that they made two much of me. They was altogether too lavish with their attenshuns.

I went amung the Seseshers with no feelins of annermosity. I went in my perfeshernal capacity. I was actooated by one of the most Loftiest desires which can swell the human Buzzum, viz: — to giv the peeple their money's worth, by showin them Sagashus Beests, and Wax Statoots, which I venter to say air onsurpast by any other statoots anywheres. I will not call that man who sez my statoots is humbugs a lier and a hoss thief, but bring him be4 me and I'll wither him with one of my scornful frowns.

But to proseed with my tail. In my travels threw the Sonny South I heared a heap of talk about Seceshon and bustin up the Union, but I didn't think it mounted to nothin. The politicians in all the villages was swearin that Old Abe (sometimes called the Prahayrie flower) should'nt never be noggerated. They also made fools of theirselves in varis ways, but as they was used to that I didn't let it worry me much, and the Stars and Stripes continued for to wave over my little tent. Moor over, I was a Son of Malty and a member of several other Temperance Societies, and my wife she was a Dawter of Malty, an I sposed these fax would secoor me the infloonz and pertectiun of all the fust families. Alas! I was dispinted. State arter State seseshed and it growed hotter and hotter for the undersined. Things came to a climbmacks in a small town in Alabamy, where I was premtorally ordered to haul down the Stars & Stripes. A deppytashun of red-faced men cum up to the door of my tent ware I was standin takin money (the arternoon exhibishun had commenst, an' my Italyun organist was jerkin his sole-stirrin chimes.) "We air cum, Sir," said a millingtary man in a cockt hat, "upon a hi and holy mishun. The Southern Eagle is screamin threwout this sunny land — proudly and defiantly screamin, Sir!'

"What's the matter with him," sez I, "don't his vittles sit well on his stummick?"

"That Eagle, Sir, will continner to scream all over this Brite and tremenjus land!"

"Wall, let him *scream*. If your Eagle can amuse hisself by screamin, let him went!" The men anoyed me for I was Bizzy makin change.

"We are cum, Sir, upon a matter of dooty — "

"You're right, Capting. It's every man's dooty to visit my show," sed I.

"We air cum — "

"And that's the reason you are here!" sez I, larfin one of my silvery larfs. I thawt if he wanted to goak I'd giv him sum of my sparklin eppygrams.

"Sir, you're inserlent. The plain question is, will you haul down the Star-Spangled Banner, and hist the Southern flag!"

"Nary hist!" Those was my reply.

"Your wax works and beests is then confisticated, & you air arrested as a Spy!"

Sez I, "My fragrant roses of the Southern clime and Bloomin daffodils, what's the price of whisky in this town, and how many cubic feet of that seductive flooid can you individooally hold?"

They made no reply to that, but said my wax figgers was confisticated. I axed them if that was ginerally the stile among thieves in that country, to which they also made no reply, but sed I was arrested as a Spy, and must go to Montgomry in iuns They was by this time jined by a large crowd of other Southern patrits, who commenst hollerin "Hang the bald-headed aberlitionist, and bust up his immoral exhibition!" I was ceased and tied to a stump, and the crowd went for my tent — that water-proof pavilion, wherein instruction and amoosment had been so muchly combined, at 15 cents per head — and tore it all to pieces. Meanwhile dirty faced boys was throwin stuns and empty beer bottles at my massiv brow, and takin other improper liberties with my person. Resistance was useless, for a variety of reasons, as I readily obsarved.

The Seseshers confisticated my statoots by smashin them to attums. They then went to my money box and confisticated all the loose change therein contaned. They then went and bust in my cages, lettin all the animils loose, a small but helthy tiger among the rest. This tiger has a excentric way of tearin dogs to peaces, and I allers sposed from his gineral conduck that he'd hav no hesitashun in servin human beins in the same way if he could git at them. Excuse me if I was crooil, but I larfed boysterrusly when I see that tiger spring in among the people. "Go it, my sweet cuss!" I inardly exclaimed, "I forgive you for bitin off my left thum with all my heart! Rip 'em up like a bully tiger whose Lare has bin inwaded by Seseshers!"

I can't say for certain that the tiger serisly injured any of them, but as he was seen a few days after, sum miles distant, with a large and well selected assortment of seats of trowsis in his mouth, and as he lookt as tho he'd bin havin sum vilent exercise, I raything guess he did. You will therefore perceive that they didn't confisticate him much.

I was carrid to Montgomry in iuns and placed in durans vial. The jail was a ornery edifiss, but the table was librally surplied with Bakin an Cabbidge. This was a good variety, for when I didn't hanker after Bakin I could help myself to the cabbige.

I had nobody to talk to nor nothin to talk about, howsever, and I was very lonely, specially on the first day; so when the jailer parst my lonely sell I put the few stray hairs on the back part of my hed

(I'm bald now, but thare was a time when I wore sweet auburn ringlets) into as dish-hevild a state as possible, & rollin my eyes like a manyyuck, I cride: "Stay, jaler, stay! I am not mad but soon shall be if you don't bring me suthin to Talk!" He brung me sum noospapers, for which I thanked him kindly.

At larst I got a interview with Jefferson Davis, the President of the Southern Conthieveracy. He was quite perlite, and axed me to sit down and state my case. I did it, when he larfed and said his gallunt men had been a little 2 enthoosiastic in confisticatin my show.

"Yes," sez I, "they confisticated me too muchly. I had sum hosses confisticated in the same way onct, but the confisticaters air now poundin stun in the States Prison in Injinnapylus."

"Wall, wall, Mister Ward, you air at liberty to depart; you air frendly to the South, I know. Even now we hav many frens in the North, who sympathise with us, and won't mingle with this fight."

"J. Davis, there's your grate mistaik. Many of

us was your sincere frends, and thought certin parties amung us was fussin about you and meddlin with your consarns intirely too much. But J. Davis, the minit you fire a gun at the piece of dry-goods called the Star-Spangled Banner, the North gits up and rises en massy, in defence of that banner. Not agin you as individooals, — not agin the South even — but to save the flag. We should indeed be weak in the knees, unsound in the heart, milk-white in the liver, and soft in the hed, if we stood quietly by and saw this glorus Govyment smashed to pieces, either by a furrin or a intestine foe. The gentle-harted mother hates to take her naughty child across her knee, but she knows it is her dooty to do it. So we shall hate to whip the naughty South, but we must do it if you don't make back tracks at onct, and we shall wallup you out of your boots! J. Davis, it is my decided opinion that the Sonny South is makin a egrejus mutton-hed of herself!"

"Go on, sir, you're safe enuff. You're too small powder for me!" sed the President of the Southern Conthieveracy.

"Wait till I go home and start out the Baldinsvill Mounted Hoss Cavalry! I'm Capting of that Corpse, I am, and J. Davis, beware! Jefferson D., I now leave you! Farewell my gay Saler Boy! Good bye, my bold buccaneer! Pirut of the deep blue sea, adoo! adoo!"

My tower threw the Southern Conthieveracy on my way home was thrillin enuff for yeller covers. It will form the subjeck of my next. Betsy Jane and the progeny air well.

Yours respectively,

A. WARD.

THRILLING SCENES IN DIXIE.

I had a narrer scape from the sonny South. "The swings and arrers of outrajus fortin," alluded to by Hamlick, warn't nothin in comparison to my trubles. I come pesky near swearin sum profane oaths more'n onct, but I hope I didn't do it, for I've promist she whose name shall be nameless (except that her initials is Betsy J.) that I'll jine the Meetin House at Baldinsville, jest as soon as I can scrape money enuff together so I can 'ford to be piuss in good stile, like my welthy nabers. But if I'm confisticated agin I'm fraid I shall continner on in my present benited state for sum time.

I figgered conspicyusly in many thrillin scenes in my tower from Montgomry to my humsted, and on sevril occasions I thought "the grate komick paper" would'nt be inriched no more with my lubrications

Arter biddin adoo to Jefferson D. I started for the depot. I saw a nigger sittin on a fence a-playin on a banjo. "My Afrikan Brother," sed I, coting from a Track I onct red, "you belong to a very interesting race. Your masters is going to war ex cloosively on your account."

"Yes, boss," he replied, "an' I wish 'em honorable graves!" and he went on playin the banjo, larfin all over and openin his mouth wide enuff to drive in an old-fashioned 2 wheeled chaise.

The train of cars in which I was to trust my wallerable life was the scaliest, rickytiest lookin lot of consarns that I ever saw on wheels afore. "What time does this string of second-hand coffins leave?" I inquired of the depot master. He sed direckly, and I went in & sot down. I hadn't more'n fairly squatted afore a dark lookin man with a swinister expression onto his countenance entered the cars, and lookin very sharp at me, he axed what was my principles?

"Secesh!" I ansered. "I'm a Dissoluter. I'm in favor of Jeff Davis, Bowregard, Pickens, Capt.

Kidd, Bloobeard, Munro Edards, the devil, Mrs. Cunningham and all the rest of 'em."

"You're in favor of the war?"

"Certingly. By all means. I'm in favor of this war and also of the next war. I've been in favor of the next war for over sixteen years!"

"War to the knive!" sed the man.

"Blud, Eargo, blud!" sed I, tho them words isn't origgernal with me. Them words was rit by Shakspeare, who is ded. His mantle fell onto the author of "The Seven Sisters," who's goin to hav a Spring overcoat made out of it.

We got under way at larst, an' proceeded on our jerney at about the rate of speed which is ginrally obsarved by properly-conducted funeral processions. A hansum yung gal, with a red musketer bar on the back side of her hed, and a sassy little black hat tipt over her forrerd, sot in the seat with me. She wore a little Sesesh flag pin'd onto her hat, and she was a goin for to see her troo-love, who had jined the Southern army, all so bold and gay. So she told me. She was chilly and I offered her my blanket.

"Father livin?" I axed.

"Yes sir."

"Got any Uncles?"

"A heap. Uncle Thomas is ded, tho."

"Peace to Uncle Thomas's ashes, and success to him! I will be your Uncle Thomas! Lean on me my pretty Secesher, and linger in Blissful repose!" She slept as secoorly as in her own housen, and didn't disturb the sollum stillness of the night with 'ary snore!

At the first station a troop of Sojers entered the cars and inquired if "Old Wax Works" was on bored. That was the disrespectiv stile in which they referred to me. "Becawz if Old Wax Works is on bored," sez a man with a face like a double-brested lobster, "we're going to hang Old Wax Works!"

"My illustrious and patriotic Bummers!" sez I, a gittin up and takin orf my Shappo, "if you allude to A. Ward, it's my pleasin dooty to inform you that he's ded. He saw the error of his ways at 15 minits parst 2 yesterday, and stabbed hisself with a stuffed sled-stake, dyin in five beautiful tabloos to slow moosic! His larst words was: 'My perfeshernal career is over! I jerk no more!' "

"And who be you?"

"I'm a stoodent in Senater Benjamin's law offiss. I'm going up North to steal some spoons and things for the Southern Army."

This was satisfactry and the intossicated troopers went orf. At the next station the pretty little Secesher awoke and sed she must git out there. I bid her a kind adoo and giv her sum pervisions. "Accept my blessin and this hunk of gingerbred!" I sed. She thankt me muchly and tript galy away. There's considerable human nater in a man, and I'm fraid I shall allers giv aid and comfort to the enemy if he cums to me in the shape of a nice young gal.

At the next station I didn't get orf so easy. I was dragged out of the cars and rolled in the mud for several minits, for the purpose of "takin the conseet out of me," as a Secesher kindly stated.

I was let up finally, when a powerful large Secesher came up and embraced me, and to show that he had no hard feelins agin me, put his nose into my mouth. I returned the compliment by placin my stummick suddenly agin his right foot, when he kindly made a spittoon of his able-bodied face. Actooated by a desire to see whether the Secesher had bin vaxinated I then fastened my teeth onto his left coat-sleeve and tore it to the shoulder. We then vilently bunted our heads together for a few minits, danced around a little, and sot down in a mud puddle. We riz to our feet agin & by a sudden and adroit movement I placed my left eye agin the Seaesher's fist. We then rushed into each other's arms and fell under a two-hoss wagon. I was very much exhaustid and didn't care about gettin up agin, but the man said he reckoned I'd better, and I conclooded I would. He pulled me up, but I hadn't bin on my feet more'n two seconds afore the ground flew up and hit me in the hed. The crowd sed it was high old sport, but I couldn't zackly see where the lafture come in. I riz and we embraced agin. We careered madly to a steep bank, when I got the upper hands of my antaggernist and threw him into the raveen. He fell about forty feet, striking a grindstone pretty hard. I understood he was injured. I haven't heard from the grindstone.

A man in a cockt hat cum up and sed he felt as though a apology was doo me. There was a mistake. The crowd had taken me for another man! I told him not to mention it, and axed him if his wife and little ones was so as to be about, and got on bored the train, which had stopped at that station "20 minits for refreshments." I got all I wantid. It was the hartiest meal I ever et.

I was rid on a rale the next day, a bunch of blazin fire crackers bein tied to my coat tales. It was a fine spectycal in a dramatic pint of view, but I didn't enjoy it. I had other adventers of a startlin kind, but why continner? Why lasserate the Public Boozum with these here things? Suffysit to say I got across Mason & Dixie's line safe at last. I made tracks for my humsted, but she to whom I'm harnist for life failed to recognize, in the emashiated bein who stood before her, the gushin youth of forty-six summers who had left her only a few months afore,

But I went into the pantry, and brought out a certin black bottle. Raisin it to my lips, I sed "Here's to you, old gal!" I did it so natral that she knowed me at once. "Those form! Them voice! That natral stile of doin things! 'Tis he!" she cried, and rushed into my arms. It was too much for her & she fell into a swoon. I cum very near swoundin myself.

No more to-day from yours for the Pepetration of the Union, and the bringin of the Goddess of Liberty out of her present bad fix.

FOURTH OF JULY ORATION.

DELIVERED JULY 4TH, AT WEATHERSFIELD, CONNECTICUT, 1859.

[I delivered the follerin, about two years ago, to a large and discriminating awjince. I was 96 minits passin a given pint. I have revised the orashun, and added sum things which makes it appropposser to the times than it otherwise would be. I have also corrected the grammers and punktooated it. I do my own punktooatin now days. The printers in VANITY FAIR offiss can't punktooate worth a cent.]

FELLER CITIZENS: I've bin honored with a invite to norate before you to-day; and when I say that I skurcely feel ekal to the task, I'm sure you will believe me.

Weathersfield is justly celebrated for her onyins and patritism the world over, and to be axed to paws and address you on this, my fust perfeshernal tower threw New Englan, causes me to feel — to feel — I may say it causes me to *feel*. (Grate applaws. They thought this was one of my eccen

Piccolomini in the "Child of the Regiment." [*See Page* 130.]

tricities, while the fact is I was stuck. This between you and I.)

I'm a plane man. I don't know nothin about no ded languages and am a little shaky on livin ones. There4, expect no flowry talk from me. What I shall say will be to the pint, right strate out.

I'm not a politician and my other habits air good. I've no enemys to reward, nor friends to sponge. But I'm a Union man. I luv the Union — it is a Big thing — and it makes my hart bleed to see a lot of ornery peple a-movin heaven — no, not heaven, but the other place — and earth, to bust it up. Too much good blud was spilt in courtin and marryin that hily respectable female the Goddess of Liberty, to git a divorce from her now. My own State of Injianny is celebrated for unhitchin marrid peple with neatness and dispatch, but you can't git a divorce from the Goddess up there. Not by no means. The old gal has behaved herself too well to cast her off now. I'm sorry the picters don't give her no shoes or stockins, but the band of stars upon her hed must continner to shine undimd, forever.

I'me for the Union as she air, and whithered be the arm of every ornery cuss who attempts to bust her up. That's me. I hav sed! [It was a very sweaty day, and at this pint of the orashun a man fell down with sunstroke. I told the awjince that considerin the large number of putty gals present I was more fraid of a DAWTER STROKE. This was impromptoo, and seemed to amoose them very much.]

Feller Citizens — I hain't got time to notis the growth of Ameriky frum the time when the Mayflowers cum over in the Pilgrim and brawt Plymmuth Rock with them, but every skool boy nose our kareer has bin tremenjis. You will excuse me if I don't prase the erly settlers of the Kolonies. Peple which hung idiotic old wimin for witches, burnt holes in Quakers' tongues and consined their feller critters to the tredmill and pillery on the slitest provocashun may hav bin very nice folks in their way, but I must confess I don't admire their stile, and will pass them by. I spose they ment well, and so, in the novel and techin langwidge of the nusepapers, "peas to their ashis." Thare was no diskount, however, on them brave men who fit, bled and died in the American Revolushun. We needn't be afraid of setting 'em up two steep. Like my show, they will stand any amount of prase. G. Washington was abowt the best man this world ever sot eyes on. He was a clear-heded, warm-harted, and stiddy goin man. He never slopt over! The prevailin weakness of most public men is to SLOP OVER! [Put them words in large letters — A. W.] They git filled up and slop. They Rush Things. They travel too much on the high presher principle. They git on to the fust poplar hobby-hoss whitch trots along, not carin a sent whether the beest is even goin, clear sited and sound or spavined, blind and bawky. Of course they git throwed eventooually, if not sooner. When they see the multitood goin it blind they go Pel Mel with it, instid of exertin theirselves to set it right. They can't see that the crowd which is now bearin them triumfuntly on its shoulders will soon diskiver its error and cast them into the hoss pond of Oblivyun, without the slitest hesitashun. Washington never slopt over. That wasn't George's stile. He luved his country dearly. He wasn't after the spiles. He was a human angil in a 3 kornerd hat and knee britches, and we shan't see his like right away. My frends, we can't all be Washington's, but we kin all be patrits & behave ourselves in a human and a Christian manner. When we see a brother goin down hill to Ruin let us not give him a push, but let us seeze rite hold of his coat-tails and draw him back to Morality.

Imagine G. Washington and P. Henry in the character of seseshers! As well fancy John Bunyan and Dr. Watts in spangled tites, doin the trapeze in a one-horse circus!

I tell you, feller-citizens, it would have bin ten dollars in Jeff Davis's pocket if he'd never bin born!

* * * * * * * *

Be shure and vote at leest once at all elecshuns. Buckle on yer Armer and go to the Poles. See two it that your naber is there. See that the kripples air provided with carriages. Go to the poles and stay all day. Bewair of the infamous lise whitch the Opposishun will be sartin to git up fur perlitical effek on the eve of eleckshun. To the poles! and when you git there vote jest as you darn please. This is a privilege we all persess, and it is 1 of the booties of this grate and free land.

I see mutch to admire in New Englan. Your gals in particklar air abowt as snug bilt peaces of Calliker as I ever saw. They air fully equal to the corn fed gals of Ohio and Injianny, and will make the bestest kind of wives. It sets my Buzzum on fire to look at 'em.

> Be still, my sole, be still,
> & you, Hart, stop cuttin up!

I like your skool houses, your meetin houses, your enterprise, gumpshun &c., but your favorit Bevridge I disgust. I allude to New England Rum. It is wuss nor the korn whisky of Injianny, which eats threw stone jugs & will turn the stummuck of the most shiftliss Hog. I seldom seek consolashun in the flowin Bole, but tother day I wurrid down some of your Rum. The fust glass indused me to sware like a infooriated trooper. On takin the secund glass I was seezed with a desire to break winders, & arter imbibin the third glass I knocht a small boy down, pickt his pocket of a New York Ledger, and wildly commenced readin Sylvanus Kobb's last Tail. Its dreffful stuff — a sort of lickwid litenin, gut up under the personal supervishun of the devil — tears men's inards all to peaces and makes their noses blossum as the Lobster. Shun it as you would a wild hyeny with a fire brand tied to his tale, and while you air abowt it you will do a first rate thing for yourself and everybody abowt you by shunnin all kinds of intoxicatin lickers. You don't need 'em no more'n a cat needs 2 tales, sayin nothin abowt the trubble and sufferin they cawse. But unless your inards air cast iron, avoid New Englan's favorite Bevrige.

My frends, I'm dun. I tear myself away from you with tears in my eyes & a pleasant oder of Onyins abowt my close. In the langwidge of Mister Catterline to the Rummuns, I go, but perhaps I shall cum back agin. Adoo, peple of Wethersfield. Be virtoous & you'll be happy!

Joe Stackpole says he can lick the Seceshers in a fair stand-up fight. [*See Page* 218.]

THE WAR FEVER IN BALDINSVILLE.

As soon as I'd recooperated my physikil system, I went over into the village. The peasantry was glad to see me. The skoolmaster sed it was cheerin to see that gigantic intelleck among 'em onct more. That's what he called me. I like the skoolmaster, and allers send him tobacker when I'm off on a travelin campane. Besides, he is a very sensible man. Such men must be encouraged.

They don't git news very fast in Baldinsville, as nothin but a plank road runs in there twice a week, and that's very much out of repair. So my nabers wasn't much posted up in regard to the wars, 'Squire Baxter sed he'd voted the dimicratic ticket for goin on forty year, and the war was a dam black republican lie. Jo. Stackpole, who kills hogs for the 'Squire, and has got a powerful muscle into his arms, sed he'd bet $5 he could lick the Crisis in a fair stand-up fight, if he wouldn't draw a knife on him. So it went — sum was for war, and sum was for peace. The skoolmaster, however, sed the Slave Oligarky must cower at the feet of the North ere a year had flowed by, or pass over his dead corpse. "Esto perpetua!" he added! "And sine qua non also!" sed I, sternly, wishing to make a impression onto the villagers. "Requiescat in pace!" sed the schoolmaster. "Too troo, too troo!" I anserd, "it's a scanderlus fact!"

The newspapers got along at last, chock full of war, and the patriotic fever fairly bust out in Baldinsville. 'Squire Baxter sed he didn't b'lieve in Coercion, not one of 'em, and could prove by a file of *Eagles of Liberty* in his garrit, that it was all a Whig lie, got up to raise the price of whisky and destroy our other liberties. But the old 'Squire got putty riley, when he heard how the rebels was cuttin up, and he sed he reckoned he should skour up his old muskit and do a little square fitin for the Old Flag, which had allers bin on the ticket *he'd* voted, and he was too old to Bolt now. The 'Squire is all right at heart, but it takes longer for him to fill his venerable Biler with steam than it used to when he was young and frisky. As I previously informed you, I am Captin of the Baldinsville Company. I riz gradooally but majesticly from drummer's Secretary to my present position. But I found the ranks wasn't full by no means, and commenced for to recroot. Havin notist a gineral desire on the part of young men who are into the Crisis to wear eppylits, I detarmined to have my company composed excloosively of offissers, everybody to rank as Brigadeer-Ginral. The follerin was among the varis questions which I put to recroots :

Do you know a masked battery from a hunk of gingerbread ?

Do you know a eppylit from a piece of chalk ?

If I trust you with a real gun, how many men of your own company do you speck you can manage to kill durin the war ?

Hav you ever heard of Ginral Price of Missouri, and can you avoid simler accidents in case of a battle ?

Hav you ever had the measles, and if so, how many?

How air you now?

Show me your tongue, &c., &c. Sum of the questions was sarcusstical.

The company filled up rapid, and last Sunday we went to the meetin house in full uniform. I had a seris time gittin into my military harness, as it was bilt for me many years ago; but I finally got inside of it, tho' it fitted me putty clost. Howsever, onct into it, I lookt fine — in fact, aw-inspirin. "Do you know me, Mrs. Ward?" sed I walkin into the kitchin.

"Know you, you old fool? Of course I do."

I saw at once she did.

I started for the meetin house, and I'm afraid I tried to walk too strate, for I cum very near fallin over backards; and in attemptin to recover myself, my sword got mixed up with my legs, and I fell in among a choice collection of young ladies, who was standin near the church door a-seein the sojer boys come up. My cockt hat fell off, and sumhow my coat tales got twisted round my neck. The young ladies put their handkerchers to their mouths and remarked: "Te he," while my ancient female single friend, Sary Peasley, bust out into a loud larf. She exercised her mouth so vilently that her new false teeth fell out onto the ground.

"Miss Peaseley," sed I, gittin up and dustin myself, "you must be more careful with them store teeth of your'n or you'll have to gum it agin!"

Methinks I had her.

I'd bin to work hard all the week, and I felt rather snoozy. I'm 'fraid I did git half asleep, for on hearin the minister ask, "Why was man made to mourn?" I sed, "I giv it up," havin a vague idee that it was a condrum. It was a onfortnit remark, for the whole meetin house lookt at me with mingled surprise and indignation. I was about risin to a pint of order, when it suddenly occurd to me whare I was, and I kept my seat, blushin like the red, red rose — so to speak.

The next mornin I 'rose with the lark (N. B. — I don't sleep with the lark, tho'. A goak.)

My little dawter was execootin ballids, accompanyin herself with the Akordeon, and she wisht me to linger and hear her sing: "Hark I hear a angel singin, a angel now is onto the wing."

"Let him fly, my child!" said I, a-bucklin on my armer, "I must forth to my Biz."

We air progressin pretty well with our drill. As all air commandin offissers, there ain't no jelusy; and as we air all exceedin smart, it t'aint worth while to try to outstrip each other. The idee of a company composed excloosively of Commanders-in-Chiefs, orriggernated, I spose I skurcely need say, in these Brane. Considered *as* a idee, I flatter myself it is putty hefty. We've got all the tackticks at our tongs' ends, but what we particly excel in is restin muskits. We can rest muskits with anybody.

Our corpse will do its dooty. We go to the aid of Columby — we fight for the stars!

We'll be chopt into sassige meat before we'll exhibit our coat-tales to the foe.

We'll fight till there's nothin left of us but our little toes, and even they shall defiantly wiggle!

"Ever of thee,"

A WARD.

INTERVIEW WITH THE PRINCE NAPOLEON.

Notwithstandin I haint writ much for the papers of late, nobody needn't flatter theirselves that the undersined is ded. On the contry, "I still live," which words was spoken by Danyil Webster, who was a able man. Even the old-line whigs of Boston will admit *that*. Webster is ded now, howsever, and his mantle has probly fallen into the hands of sum dealer in 2nd hand close, who can't sell it. Leastways nobody pears to be goin round wearin it to any perticler extent, now days. The rigiment of whom I was kurnel, finerly concluded they was better adapted as Home Gards, which accounts for your not hearin of me, ear this, where the bauls is the thickest and where the cannon doth roar. But as a American citizen I shall never cease to admire the masterly advance our troops made on Washington from Bull

Run, a short time ago. It was well dun. I spoke to my wife 'bout it at the time. My wife sed it was well dun.

It havin there4 bin detarmined to pertect Baldinsville at all hazzuds, and as there was no apprehensions of any immejit danger, I thought I would go orf onto a pleasure tower. Accordinly I put on a clean Biled Shirt and started for Washinton. I went there to see the Prints Napoleon, and not to see the place, which I will here take occasion to obsarve is about as uninterestin a locality as there is this side of J. Davis's future home, if he ever does die, and where I reckon they'll make it so warm for him that he will si for his summer close. It is easy enough to see why a man goes to the poor house or the penitentiary. It's becawz he can't help it. But why he should woluntarily go and live in Washinton, is intirely beyond my comprehension, and I can't say no fairer nor that.

I put up to a leadin hotel. I saw the landlord and sed, "How d'ye do, Square?"

"Fifty cents, sir" was his reply.

"Sir?"

"Half-a-dollar. We charge twenty-five cents for *lookin* at the landlord and fifty cents for speakin to him. If you want supper, a boy will show you to the dinin room for twenty-five cents. Your room bein in the tenth story, it will cost you a dollar to be shown up there."

"How much do you ax a man for breathin in this equinomikal tarvun?" sed I.

"Ten cents a Breth," was his reply.

Washinton hotels is very reasonable in their charges. [N. B.—This is Sarkassum.]

I sent up my keerd to the Prints, and was immejitly ushered before him. He received me kindly, and axed me to sit down.

"I hav cum to pay my respecks to you, Mister Napoleon, hopin I see you hale and harty."

"I am quite well," he sed. "Air you well, sir?"

"Sound as a cuss!" I answerd.

He seemed to be pleased with my ways, and we entered into ccnversation to onct.

"How's Lewis?" I axed, and he sed the Emperor was well. Eugeny was likewise well, he sed. Then I axed him was Lewis a good provider? did he cum home arly nites? did he perfoom her bedroom at a onseasonable hour with gin and tanzy? Did he go to "the Lodge" on nites when there wasn't any Lodge? did he often hav to go down town to meet a friend? did he hav a extensiv acquaintance among poor young widders whose husbands was in Californy? to all of which questions the Prints perlitely replide, givin me to understan that the Emperor was behavin well.

"I ax these questions, my royal duke and most noble higness and imperials, becaws I'm anxious to know how he stands as a man. I know he's smart. He is cunnin, he is long-heded, he is deep — he is grate. But onless he is *good* he'll come down with a crash one of these days and the Bonyparts will be Bustid up agin. Bet yer life!"

"Air you a preacher, sir?" he inquired, slitely sarkasticul.

"No, sir. But I bleeve in morality. I likewise

bleeve in Meetin Houses. Show me a place where there isn't any Meetin Houses and where preachers is never seen, and I'll show you a place where old hats air stuffed into broken winders, where the children air dirty and ragged, where gates have no hinges, where the wimin are slipshod, and where maps of the devil's "wild land" air painted upon men's shirt-bosums with tobacco-jooce! That's what I'll show you. Let us consider what the preachers do for us before we aboose 'em."

He sed he didn't mean to aboose the clergy. Not at all, and he was happy to see that I was interested in the Bonypart family.

"It's a grate family," sed I. "But they scooped the old man in."

"How, sir?"

"Napoleon the Grand. The Britishers scooped him at Waterloo. He wanted to do too much, and he did it! They scooped him in at Waterloo, and he subsekently died at St. Heleny! There's where the gratest military man this world ever projuced pegged out. It was rather hard to consine such a man as him to St. Heleny, to spend his larst days in catchin mackeril, and walkin up and down the dreary beach in a military cloak drawn titely round him, (see picter-books), but so it was. 'Hed of the Army!' Them was his larst words. So he had bin. He was grate! Don't I wish we had a pair of his old boots to command sum of our Brigades!"

This pleased Jerome, and he took me warmly by the hand.

"Alexander the Grate was punkins," I continnered, but Napoleon was punkinser! Alic. wept becaws there was no more worlds to scoop, and then took to drinkin. He drowndid his sorrers in the flowin bole, and the flowin bole was too much for him. It ginerally is. He undertook to give a snake exhibition in his boots, but it killed him. That was a bad joke on Alic!"

"Since you air so solicitous about France and the Emperor, may I ask you how your own country is getting along?" sed Jerome, in a pleasant voice.

"It's mixed," I sed. "But I think we shall cum out all right."

"Columbus, when he diskivered this magnificent continent, could hav had no idee of the grandeur it would one day assoom," sed the Prints.

It cost Columbus twenty thousand dollars to fit out his explorin expedition," sed I. "If he had bin a sensible man he'd hav put the money in a hoss railroad or a gas company, and left this magnificent continent to intelligent savages, who when they got hold of a good thing knew enuff to keep it, and who wouldn't hav seceded, nor rebelled, nor knockt Liberty in the hed with a slungshot. Columbus wasn't much of a feller, after all. It would hav bin money in my pocket if he'd staid to home. Chris. ment well, but he put his foot in it when he saled for America."

We talked sum more about matters and things, and at larst I riz to go. "I will now say good bye to you, noble sir, and good luck to you. Likewise the same to Clotildy. Also to the gorgeous persons which compose your soot. If the Emperor's boy don't like livin at the Tooleries, when he gits older, and would like to imbark in the show bizniss, let him come with me and I'll make a man of him. You find us sumwhat mixed, as I before obsarved, but come again next year and you'll find us clearer nor ever. The American Eagle has lived too sumptuously of late — his stummic becum foul, and he's takin a slite emetic. That's all. We're gettin ready to strike a big blow and a sure one. When we do strike the fur will fly and secession will be in the hands of the undertaker, sheeted for so deep a grave that nothin short of Gabriel's trombone will ever awaken it! Mind what I say. You've heard the showman!"

Then advisin him to keep away from the Peter Funk auctions of the East, and the proprietors of corner-lots in the West, I bid him farewell, and went away.

There was a levee at Senator What's-his-name's, and I thought I'd jine in the festivities for a spell. Who should I see but she that was Sarah Watkins, now the wife of our Congresser, trippin in the dance, dressed up to kill in her store close. Sarah's father use to keep a little grosery store in our town and she used to clerk it for him in busy times. I was rushin up to shake hands with her when she turned on her heel, and tossin her hed in a contemptooious manner, walked away from me very rapid. "Hallo, Sal," I hollered, "can't you measure me a quart of them best melasses? I may want a codfish, also!" I guess this reminded her of the little red store, and "the days of her happy childhood."

But I fell in with a nice little gal after that, who was much sweeter than Sally's father's melasses, and I axed her if we shouldn't glide in the messy dance. She sed we should, and we Glode.

I intended to make this letter very seris, but a few goaks may have accidentally crept in. Never mind. Besides, I think it improves a komick paper to publish a goak once in a while.

Yours Muchly,

WARD, (Artemus.)

18

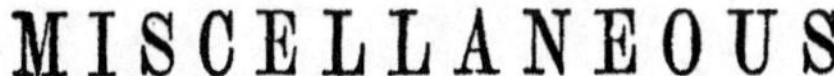
MISCELLANEOUS

MARION:

A ROMANCE OF THE FRENCH SCHOOL.

I.

——, Friday, ——, 1860.

On the sad sea shore! Always to hear the moaning of these dismal waves!

Listen. I will tell you my story — my story of love, of misery, of black despair.

I am a moral Frenchman.

She whom I adore, whom I adore still, is the wife of a fat Marquis — a lop-eared, blear-eyed, greasy Marquis. A man without soul. A man without sentiment, who cares naught for moonlight and music. A low, practical man, who pays his debts. I hate him.

II.

She, my soul's delight, my empress, my angel, is superbly beautiful.

I loved her at first sight — devotedly, madly.

She dashed past me in her coupè. I saw her but a moment — perhaps only an instant — but she took me captive then and there, forevermore.

Forevermore !

I followed her, after that, wherever she went. At length she came to notice, to smile upon me My motto was *en avant!* That is a French word I got it out of the back part of Worcester's Dic tionary.

III.

She wrote me that I might come and see her at her own house. Oh, joy, joy unutterable, to see her at her own house !

I went to see her after nightfall, in the soft moon-light.

She came down the graveled walk to meet me, on

this beautiful midsummer night — came to me in pure white, her golden hair in splendid disorder — strangely beautiful, yet in tears!

She told me her fresh grievances.

The Marquis, always a despot, had latterly misused her most vilely.

That very morning, at breakfast, he had cursed the fishballs and sneered at the pickled onions.

She is a good cook. The neighbors will tell you so. And to be told by the base Marquis — a man who, previous to his marriage, had lived at the cheap eating-houses — to be told by him that her manner of frying fishballs was a failure — it was too much.

Her tears fell fast. I too wept. I mixed my sobs with her'n. "Fly with me!" I cried.

Her lips met mine. I held her in my arms. I felt her breath upon my cheek! It was Hunkey.

"Fly with me. To New York! I will write romances for the Sunday papers — real French romances, with morals to them. My style will be appreciated. Shop girls and young mercantile persons will adore it, and I will amass wealth with my ready pen.

Ere she could reply — ere she could articulate her ecstacy, her husband, the Marquis, crept snake-like upon me.

Shall I write it? He kicked me out of the garden — he kicked me into the street.

I did not return. How could I? I, so ethereal, so full of soul, of sentiment, of sparkling originality! He, so gross, so practical, so lop-eared!

Had I returned, the creature would have kicked me again.

So I left Paris for this place — this place, so lonely, so dismal.

Ah me!

Oh dear!

THE END.

"HOME GUARD DRILL." [*See Page* 241.]

TOUCHING LETTER FROM A GORY MEMBER OF THE HOME GUARD.

—— Broadway, *Dec.* 10, '61.

Dear Father and Mother:

We are getting along very well. We mess at Delmonico's. Do not repine for your son. Some must suffer for the glorious Stars and Stripes, and, dear parents, why shouldn't I? Tell Mrs. Skuller that we do not need the blankets she so kindly sent to us, as we bunk at the St. Nicholas and Metropolitan. What our brave lads stand most in need of now, is Fruit Cake and Waffles. Do not weep for me.

Henry Adolphus.

EAST SIDE THEATRICALS.

The Broadway houses have given the public immense quantities of Central Park, Seven Sisters, Nancy Sykes and J. Cade. I suppose the Broadway houses have done this chiefly because it has paid them, and so I mean no disrespect when I state that to me the thing became rather stale. I sighed for novelty. A man may stand stewed veal for several years, but banquets consisting exclusively of stewed veal would become uninteresting after a century or so. A man would want something else. The least particular man, it seems to me, would desire to have his veal "biled," by way of a change. So I, tired of the thread-bare pieces at the Broadway houses, went to the East Side for something fresh. I wanted to see some libertines and brigands. I wanted to see some cheerful persons identified with the blacksmith and sewing-machine interests triumph over those libertines and brigands, in the most signal manner. I wanted, in short, to see the Downfall of Vice and Triumph of Virtue. That was what ailed me. And so I went to the East Side.

Poor Jack Scott is gone, and Jo. Kirby dies no more on the East Side. They've got the blood and things over there, but alas! they're deficient in lungs. The tragedians in the Bowery and Chatham street of to-day dont start the shingles on the roof as their predecessors, now cold and stiff in death, used to when they threw themselves upon their knees at the footlights and roared a redhot curse after the lord who had carried Susan away, swearing to never more eat nor drink until the lord's vile heart was torn from his body, and ther-rown to the dorgs — rattling their knives against the tin lamps and glaring upon the third tier most fearfully the while.

Glancing at the spot where it is said Senator Benjamin used to vend second-hand clothes, and regretting that he had not continued in that comparatively honorable vocation instead of sinking to his present position; — wondering if Jo. Kirby would ever consent, if he were alive, to die wrapped up in a Secession flag! — gazing admiringly upon the unostentatious sign-board which is suspended in front of the Hon. Izzy Lazarus's tavern; — glancing, wondering and gazing thus, I enter the Old Chatham theatre. The pit is full, but people fight shy of the boxes.

The play is about a servant-girl, who comes to the metropolis from the agricultural districts, in short skirts, speckled hose, and a dashing little white hat, gaily decked with pretty pink ribbons — that being the style of dress invariably worn by servant-girls from the interior. She is accompanied by a chaste young man in a short-tailed red coat, who, being very desirous of protecting her from the temptations of a large city, naturally leaves her in the street and goes off somewhere. Servant-girl encounters an elderly female, who seems to be a very nice sort of person indeed, but the young man in a short-tailed coat comes in and thrusts the elderly female aside, calling her "a vile hag." This pleases the pit, which is ever true to virtue, and it accordingly cries "Hi! hi! hi!"

A robber appears. The idea of a robber in times like these, is rather absurd. The most adroit robber would eke out a miserable subsistence if he attempted to follow his profession now-a-days. I should prefer to publish a daily paper in Chelsea. Nevertheless, here is a robber. He has been playing poker with his "dupe," but singularly enough the dupe has won all the money. This displeases the robber, and it occurs to him that he will kill the dupe. He accordingly sticks him. The dupe staggers, falls, says "Dearest Eliza!" and dies. Cries of hi! hi! hi!" in the pit, while a gentleman with a weed on his hat, in the boxes, states that the price of green smelts is five cents a quart. This announcement is not favorably received by the pit, several members of which come back at the weeded individual with some advice in regard to liquidating a long-standing account for beans and other refreshments at an adjacent restaurant.

The robber is seized with remorse, and says the money which he has taken from the dupe's pockets, "scorches" him. Robber seeks refuge in a miser's drawing-room, where he stays for "seven days." There is a long chest, full of money and diamonds in the room. The chest is unlocked, but misers very frequently go off and leave long chests full of money unlocked in their drawing rooms, for seven days; and this robber was too much of a gentleman to take advantage of this particular miser's absence. By-and-by the miser returns, when the robber quietly kills him and chucks him in the chest. "Sleep with your gold, old man!" says the bold robber, as he melodramatically retreats — retreats to a cellar, where the servant girl resides. Finds that she was formerly his gal, when he resided in the rural districts, and regrets having killed so many persons, for if so be he hadn't he might marry her and settle down, whereas now he can't do it, as he says he is "unhappy." But he gives her a ring — a ring he had stolen from the dupe — and flies. Presently the dupe, who has come to life in a singular

One of the Broadway "Seven Sisters." [*See Page* 242.]

but eminently theatrical manner, is brought into the cellar. He discovers the ring upon the servant girl's finger — servant girl states that she is innocent, and the dupe, with the remark that he sees his mother, dies, this time positively without reserve. Servant girl is taken to Newgate, whither goes the robber and gains admission by informing the turnkey that he is her uncle. Throws off his disguise, and like a robber bold and gay, says he is the guilty party and will save the servant girl. He drinks a vial of poison, says he sees *his* mother, and dies to slow fiddling. Servant girl throws herself upon him wildly, and the virtuous young party in a short-tailed coat comes in and assists in the tableau. Robber tells the servant girl to take the party in the short-tailed coat and be happy — repeats that he sees his mother (they always do). and dies again. Cries of "Hi! hi! hi!" and the weeded gentleman reiterates the price of green smelts.

Not a remarkably heavy plot, but quite as bulky as the plots of the Broadway sensation pieces.

SOLILOQUY OF A LOW THIEF.

My name is Jim Griggins. I'm a low thief. My parients was ignorant folks, and as poor as the shadder of a bean pole. My advantages for gettin' a eddycation was exceedin' limited. I growed up in the street, quite loose and permiskis, you see, and took to vice because I had nothing else to take to, and because nobody had never given me a sight at virtue.

I'm in the penitentiary. I was sent here onct before for priggin' a watch. I served out my time, and now I'm here agin, this time for stealin' a few insignificant clothes.

I shall always blame my parients for not eddycatin' me. Had I bin liberally eddycated I could, with my brilliant native talents, have bin a big thief — I b'leeve they call 'em defaulters. Instead of confinin' myself to priggin' clothes, watches, spoons and sich like, I could have plundered princely sums — thousands and hundreds of thousands of dollars — and that old humbug, the law, wouldn't have harmed a hair of my head! For, you see, I should be smart enough to get elected State Treasurer, or have something to do with Banks or Railroads, and perhaps a little of both. Then, you see, I could ride in my carriage, live in a big house with a free stun frunt, drive a fast team, and drink as much gin and sugar as I wanted. A inwestigation might be made, and some of the noosepapers might come down on me heavy, but what the d—l would I care about that, havin' previously taken precious good care of the stolen money? Besides, my "party" would swear stout that I was as innersunt as the new-born babe, and a great many people would wink very pleasant, and say, "Well, Griggins understands what *he's* 'bout, HE does!"

But havin' no eddycation, I'm only a low thief — a stealer of watches and spoons and sich — a low wretch, anyhow — and the Law puts me through without mercy.

It's all right, I s'pose, and yet I sometimes think it's wery hard to be shut up here, a wearin' checkered clothes, a livin' on cold vittles, a sleepin' on iron beds, a lookin' out upon the world through iron muskeeter bars, and poundin' stun like a galley slave, day after day, week after week, and year after year, while my brother thieves (for to speak candid, there's no difference between a thief and a defaulter, except that the latter is forty times wuss) who have stolen thousands of dollars to my one cent, are walkin' out there in the bright sunshine — dressed up to kill, new clothes upon their backs and piles of gold in their pockets! But the Law don't tech 'em. They are too big game for the Law to shoot at. It's as much as the Law can do to take care of us ignorant thieves.

Who said there was no difference 'tween tweedledum and tweedledee? He lied in his throat, like a villain as he was! I tell ye there's a tremendous difference.

Oh that I had been liberally eddycated!

JIM GRIGGINS.

SING-SING, 1860.

SURRENDER OF CORNWALLIS.

It was customary in many of the inland towns of New England, some thirty years ago, to celebrate the anniversary of the surrender of Lord Cornwallis, by a sham representation of that important event in the history of the Revolutiouary War. A town meeting would be called, at which a company of men would be detailed as British, and a company as Americans — two leading citizens being selected to represent Washington and Cornwallis in the mimic surrender.

The pleasant little town of W——, in whose schools the writer has been repeatedly "corrected," upon whose ponds he has often skated; upon whose richest orchards he has, with other juvenile bandits, many times dashed in the silent midnight; the town of W——, where it was popularly believed these bandits would "come to a bad end," resolved tc celebrate the surrender. Rival towns had celebrated, and W—— determined to eclipse them in the most signal manner. It is my privilege to tell how W—— succeeded in this determination.

The great day came. It was ushered in by the roar of musketry, the ringing of the village church bell, the squeaking of fifes, and the rattling of drums.

People poured into the village from all over the county. Never had W—— experienced such a jam. Never had there been such an onslaught upon gingerbread carts. Never had New England rum (for this was before Neal Dow's day) flowed so freely. And W——'s fair daughters, who mounted the house-tops to see the surrender, had never looked fairer. The old folks came, too, and among them were several war, scarred heroes, who had fought gallantly at Monmouth and Yorktown. These brave sons of '76 took no part in the demonstration, but an honored bench was set apart for their exclusive use on the piazza of Sile Smith's store. When they were dry, all they had to do was to sing out to Sile's boy, Jerry, "a leetle New Englan' this way, if *you* please." It was brought forthwith.

At precisely 9 o'clock, by the schoolmaster's new "Lepeen" watch, the American and British forces marched on to the village green and placed themselves in battle array, reminding the spectator of the time when

> "Brave Wolf drew up his men
> In a style most pretty,
> On the Plains of Abraham
> Before the city."

The character of Washington had been assigned to 'Squire Wood, a well-to-do and influential farmer, while that of Cornwallis had been given to the village lawyer, a kind-hearted but rather pompous person, whose name was Caleb Jones.

'Squire Wood, the Washington of the occasion, had met with many unexpected difficulties in preparing his forces, and in his perplexity he had emptied not only his own canteen but those of most of his aids. The consequence was — mortifying as it must be to all true Americans — blushing as I do to tell it, Washington at the commencement of the mimic struggle was most unqualifiedly drunk.

The sham fight commenced. Bang! bang! bang! from the Americans — bang! bang! bang! from the British. The bangs were kept hotly up until the powder gave out, and then came the order to charge. Hundreds of wooden bayonets flashed fiercly in the sunlight, each soldier taking very good care not to hit any body.

"Thaz (hic) right," shouted Washington, who during the shooting had been racing his horse wildly up and down the line, "thaz right! *Gin* it to 'em! Cut their tarnal heads off!"

"On Romans!" shrieked Cornwallis, who had once seen a theatrical performance and remembered the heroic appeals of the Thespian belligerents, "on to the fray! No sleep till mornin'."

"Let eout all their bowels," yelled Washington, "and down with taxation on tea!"

The fighting now ceased, the opposing forces were properly arranged, and Cornwallis, dismounting, prepared to present his sword to Washington according to programme. As he walked slowly towards the Father of His Country he rehearsed the little speech he had committed for the occasion, while the illustrious being who was to hear it was making desperate efforts to keep in his saddle. Now he would wildly brandish his sword and narrowly escape cutting off his horse's ears, and then he would fall suddenly forward on to the steed's neck, grasping the mane as drowning men seize hold of straws. He was giving an inimitable representation of Toodles on horseback. All idea of the magnitude of the occasion had left him, and when he saw Cornwallis approaching, with slow and stately step, and sword-hilt extended toward him he inquired,

"What-'n devil *you* want, any (hic) how!"

"General Washington," said Cornwallis, in dignified and impressive tones, "I tender you my sword. I need not inform you, Sir, how deeply —

The speech was here cut suddenly short by Washington, who driving the spurs into his horse, playfully attempted to run over the commander of the British forces. He was not permitted to do this, for his aids, seeing his unfortunate condition, seized the horse by the bridle, straightened Washington up in his saddle, and requested Cornwallis to proceed with his remarks.

"General Washington," said Cornwallis, "the British Lion prostrates himself at the feet of the American Eagle!"

"*Eagle?* EAGLE!" yelled the infuriated Washington, rolling off his horse and hitting Cornwallis a frightful blow on the head with the flat of his sword, "do you call me a *Eagle*, you mean sneakin' cuss?" He struck him again, sending him to the ground, and said, "I'll learn you to call me a Eagle, you infernal scoundrel!"

Cornwallis remained upon the ground only a moment. Smarting from the blows he had received, he arose with an entirely unlooked for recuperation on the part of the fallen, and in direct defiance of historical example; in spite of the men of both nations, indeed, he whipped the Immortal Washington until he roared for mercy.

The Americans, at first mortified and indignant at the conduct of their chief, now began to sympathize with, him and resolved to whip their mock foes in earnest. They rushed fiercely upon them, but the British were really the stronger party and drove the Americans back. Not content with this they charged madly upon them and drove them from the field — from the village, in fact. There were many heads damaged, eyes draped in mourning, noses fractured and legs lamed — it is a wonder that no one was killed outright.

Washington was confined to his house for several weeks, but he recovered at last. For a time there was a coolness between himself and Cornwallis, but they finally concluded to join the whole county in laughing about the surrender.

They live now. Time, the "artist," has thoroughly white-washed their heads, but they are very jolly still. On town meeting days the old 'Squire always rides down to the village. In the hind part of his venerable yellow wagon is always a bunch of hay, ostensibly for the old white horse, but really to hide a glass bottle from the vulgar gaze. This bottle has on one side a likeness of Lafayette, and upon the other may be seen the Goddess of Liberty. What the bottle contains inside I cannot positively say, but it is true that 'Squire Wood and Lawyer Jones visit that bottle very frequently on town meeting days and come back looking quite red in the face. When this redness in the face becomes of the blazing kind, as it generally does by the time the polls close, a short dialogue like this may be heard :

"We shall never play surrender again, Lawyer Jones!"

"Them days is over, 'Squire Wood!"

And then they laugh and jocosely punch each other in the ribs.

THE WIFE.

> Home they brought her warrior dead:
> She nor swooned, nor uttered cry:
> All her maidens, watching, said,
> "She must weep or she will die."

The propriety of introducing a sad story like the following, in a book intended to be rather cheerful in its character, may be questioned; but it so beautifully illustrates the firmness of woman when grief and despair have taken possession of "the chambers of her heart," that we cannot refrain from relating it.

Lucy M—— loved with all the ardor of a fond and faithful wife, and when he upon whom she had so confidingly leaned was stolen from her by death, her friends and companions said Lucy would go mad. Ah, how little they knew her!

Gazing for the last time upon the clay-cold features of her departed husband, this young widow — beautiful even in her grief: so ethereal to look upon and yet so firm! — looking for the last time upon the dear, familiar face, now cold and still in death — Oh, looking for the last, last time — she rapidly put on her bonnet, and thus addressed the sobbing gentlemen who were to act as pall-bearers: "You pall-bearers just go into the buttery and get some rum, and we'll start this man right along!"

A JUVENILE COMPOSITION.

ON THE ELEPHANT.

The Elephant is the most largest Annymile in the whole world. He eats hay and kakes. You must not giv the Elephant Tobacker, becoz if you do he will stamp his grate big feet upon to you and kill you fatally Ded. Some folks thinks the Elephant is the most noblest Annymile in the world, but as for Me giv Me the American Egil and the Stars & Stripes. Alexander Pottles his Peace.

20*

A POEM BY THE SAME.

SOME VERSES SUGESTID BY 2 OF MY UNCLES

Uncle Simon he
Clum up a tree
To see what he could see
When presentlee
Uncle Jim
Clum up beside of him
And squatted down by he.

THE END.

A LIST OF

BOOKS

ISSUED BY

CARLETON, PUBLISHER,

(LATE RUDD & CARLETON,)

413 Broadway,

NEW YORK.

Love (L'Amour).
A remarkable and celebrated volume on Love, translated from the French of M. J. Michelet, by Dr. J. W. Palmer, $1.00.

Woman (La Femme).
A continuation of "Love (L'Amour)," by same author, $1.00.

The Sea (La Mer).
New work by Michelet, author "Love" and "Woman," $1.00.

The Moral History of Women.
Companion to Michelet's "L'Amour," from the French, $1.00.

Mother Goose for Grown Folks.
A *brochure* of humorous and satirical rhymes for old folks, based upon the famous "Mother Goose Melodies," illustrated, 75 cts.

The Adventures of Verdant Green.
A rollicking humorous novel of English College life and experiences at Oxford University, with nearly 200 illus., $1.00.

The Old Merchants of New York.
Being entertaining reminiscences and recollections of ancient mercantile New York City, by "Walter Barrett, clerk," $1.50.

The Culprit Fay.
Joseph Rodman Drake's faery poem, elegantly printed, 50 cts.

Doctor Antonio.
One of the very best love-tales of Italian life ever published, by G. Ruffini, author of "Lorenzo Benoni," etc., etc., $1.25.

Lavinia.
A new love-story, by the author of "Doctor Antonio," $1.25.

Dear Experience.
An amusing Parisian novel, by author "Doctor Antonio," $1.00.

The Life of Alexander Von Humboldt.
A new and popular biography of this *savant*, including his travels and labors, with an introduction by Bayard Taylor, $1.25.

The Private Correspondence of Von Humboldt
With Varnhagen Von Ense and other European celebrities, $1.25.

Artemus Ward.
The best writings of this humorous author—illustrations, $1.00.

Beatrice Cenci.
An historical novel by F. D. Guerrazzi, from the Italian, $1.25

Isabella Orsini.
An historical novel by the author of "Beatrice Cenci," $1.25.

The Spirit of Hebrew Poetry.
A new theological work by Isaac Taylor, author "History of Enthusiasm," etc.—introduction by Wm. Adams D.D., $2.00.

Cesar Birotteau.

The first of a series of selections from the best French novels of Honore de Balzac. Translated from the latest Paris editions by O. W. Wight and Frank B. Goodrich ("Dick Tinto"), $1.00.

Petty Annoyances of Married Life.

The second of the series of Balzac's best French novels, $1.00

The Alchemist.

The third of the series of Balzac's best French novels, $1.00.

Eugenie Grandet.

The fourth of the series of Balzac's best French novels, $1.00.

The National School for the Soldier.

An elementary work for the soldier; teaching by questions and answers, thorough military tactics, by Capt. Van Ness, 50 cts.

The Partisan Leader.

The notorious Disunion novel, published at the South many years ago—then suppressed—now reprinted, 2 vols. in 1, $1.00.

A Woman's thoughts about Women.

A new and one of her best works, by Miss Mulock, author of "John Halifax, Gentleman," "A Life for a Life," etc., $1.00.

Ballad of Babie Bell.

Together with other poems by Thomas Bailey Aldrich, 75 cts.

The Course of True Love

Never did run smooth, a poem by Thomas B. Aldrich, 50 cts.

Poems of a Year.

By Thomas B. Aldrich, author of "Babie Bell," &c., 75 cts.

Curiosities of Natural History.

An entertaining and gossiping volume on beasts, birds, and fishes, by F. T. Buckland; two series, ea. sold separately, $1.25.

The Diamond Wedding.

And other miscellaneous poems, by Edmund C. Stedman, 75 cts.

The Prince's Ball.

A satirical poem by E. C. Stedman, with illustrations, 50 cts.

A Life of Hugh Miller.

Author of "Testimony of the Rocks," &c., new edition, $1.25.

Eric; or, Little by Little.

A capital tale of English school-life, by F. W. Farrar, $1.00.

Lola Montez.

Her lectures and autobiography, steel portrait, new ed., $1.25.

John Doe and Richard Roe.

A novel of New York city life, by Edward S. Gould, $1.00

Tom Tiddler's Ground.
Charles Dickens's Christmas Story for 1861, paper cover, 25 cts.

National Hymns.
An essay by Richard Grant White. 8vo. embellished, $1.00.

George Brimley.
Literary essays reprinted from the British Quarterlies, $1.25.

The Kelly's and the O'Kelly's.
Novel by Anthony Trollope, author of "Doctor Thorne," $1.25

General Nathaniel Lyon.
The life and political writings of this patriot soldier, $1.00

Twenty Years Around the World.
A volume of travel by John G. Vassar, Poughkeepsie, $2.50.

Philip Thaxter.
A new American novel, one vol. 12mo., cloth bound, $1.00.

Nothing to Wear.
A satirical poem by Wm. A. Butler, with illustrations, 50 cts.

Vernon Grove.
A novel by Mrs. Caroline H. Glover, Charleston, S. C., $1.00.

The Book of Chess Literature.
A complete Encyclopædia of this subject, by D. W. Fiske, $1.50.

From Haytime to Hopping.
A novel by the author of "Our Farm of Four Acres," $1.00.

The Afternoon of Unmarried Life.
An interesting theme admirably treated, new edition, $1.25.

Fast Day Sermons
Of 1861, the best Sermons by the prominent Divines, $1.25.

A Guide to Washington.
A complete hand-book for the National Capitol, illus., $1.00.

Doesticks' Letters.
The original letters of this great humorist, illustrated, $1.25

Plu-ri-bus-tah.
A comic history of America, by "Doesticks," illus., $1.25.

The Elephant Club.
A humorous view of club-life, by "Doesticks," illus., $1.25.

The Witches of New York.
Comic adventures among fortune tellers, by "Doesticks," $1.25

Like and Unlike.
A novel by A. S. Roe, author of "I've been Thinking," &c., $1.25.

The Morgesons.
A clever novel of American life, by Mrs. R. H. Stoddard, $1.00.

www.ingramcontent.com/pod-product-compliance
Lightning Source LLC
LaVergne TN
LVHW010237110826
845151LV00004B/1319

* 9 7 8 1 4 2 5 5 2 4 6 1 6 *